THE NORTHERN GARD... LIBRARY

W9-COL-289

Container
Gardening

Published by Linden Hills Press

Trade distribution by Voyageur Press
P.O. Box 338
Stillwater, MN 55082

Page Layout and Assembly by Anderberg-Lund Printing Company
Printed and bound in the United States by
Anderberg-Lund Printing Company

ISBN 0-9628378-3-0

Acknowledgement

The publisher is grateful to the following persons for their continued support of this series: Dorothy Johnson for her help even while planning the move into the new MSHS building, Jodi Lind-Hohman for her illustrations and plant knowledge, Jack Anderberg for contributing his resources, and all the contributors to the *Minnesota Horticulturist* for their love of gardening and the ability and desire to share their love and knowledge of gardening with the rest of us.

Thank you,
David Hohman
Publisher

Photo Credits

Cover - H. Lambert; page 4 - D. Emerson; page 8 - Dave Johnson; page 28 - T. Yockey; page 47 - National Garden; page 52 - D. Johnson; page 76 - D. Brown; page 90 - D. Emerson

Table of Contents

Chapter 1: Garden Types

Chapter 2: Tips and Techniques

Chapter 3: Plants for Containers

Chapter 4: Container Gardening for All Seasons

Chapter 5: Appendices

Foreword

The Northern Gardener's Library is based upon articles originally published in *Minnesota Horticulturist* magazine. Trusted as a reliable resource to northern horticulture for more than 100 years, *Minnesota Horticulturist* is the oldest continuously-published periodical in Minnesota. The official publication of the Minnesota State Horticultural Society (MSHS), *Minnesota Horticulturist* began relating experiences of horticulturists who moved to Minnesota to help feed the growing population. These pioneers faced unexpected challenges attempting to grow the fruits and vegetables they brought from Europe and the Eastern United States.

Minnesota Horticulturist has evolved to meet the needs of amateur horticulturists – gardeners who enjoy their hobby within small or large home grounds. Writers share their own experiences, which bring research and experimentation to a practical level in the home garden.

This book shares the experience of seasoned gardeners, many of whom write regularly for *Minnesota Horticulturist*. Their practical advice is based upon observations, trials and successes. Care has been taken to explain environmentally-conscious techniques and growing practices.

Two volumes in the Northern Gardener's Library series are being published in 1992: *Container Gardening* and *Landscaping with Trees & Shrubs*. The first two volumes were published in 1991: *The Good Gardener* and *Flower Gardens*. Future volumes will feature other popular horticultural themes.

All volumes in the series concentrate on the unique needs and challenges of growing home gardens in the lovely, but often harsh, climates of the northern states and Canada. Written for hardiness Zones 3 and 4, the information on culture and varieties is also valuable for Zone 5 gardens.

Introduction

What better way to face a short growing season than with colorful and productive container gardens? *Minnesota Horticulturist* magazine has assisted novice and experienced gardeners to create wonderful container gardens for many years, with planting guides, container construction, and special techniques to assure success. Our new book, *Container Gardening*, brings the best of these ideas to you. Use these compact gardens as part of your balcony, deck, patio, or condominium landscape, creating a pleasing focal point to view from inside and out.

We have decided to enlarge the scope of this book by including valuable information on gardening in raised beds. Raised beds are larger versions of patio planters and many of our recommendations for soil, plants to grow, and tips for special care are appropriate for this popular garden style.

What can you grow in containers and raised beds? Learn the many vegetables, flowers, and fruits which thrive on balconies, decks, and patios in northern gardens. *Container Gardening* includes a section on tropical plants in the northern landscape, plus ideas for planting a trellis and creating lush hanging baskets.

Whether you are a novice or an expert this book has something for you. Be ready to step into a whole new gardening adventure with *Container Gardening*.

> Dorothy B. Johnson
> Executive Director
> Minnesota State Horticultural Society

P.S. While several of the articles contain culture and growing techniques, there was simply not enough room to include all the basics needed for successful growing. For more information, refer to *The Good Gardener*, another volume in The Northern Gardener's Library Series.

THE NORTHERN GARDENER'S LIBRARY

Chapter 1

Garden Types

Balconies, Decks, and Patios

Condo Gardens

Trellis Gardens

Raised Bed Gardening

Growing Vegetables in Containers

Balconies, Decks, and Patios

Diane Emerson

f you think gardening on a balcony, patio, or deck means putting out a couple of hanging baskets and a potted geranium, you haven't seen Sis and Erwin Kelm's balcony. Sis Kelm has been an avid gardener most of her life. When she moved to Minneapolis nine years ago with her husband, Erwin, they decided to buy a condominium overlooking Lake Calhoun. Despite the lack of a yard, Sis refused to be without a garden. She set about creating a garden on their balcony, five stories up. Whether your plans for container gardening are high in the sky or more down to earth, the Kelm's balcony garden offers inspiration and good advice.

High-rise gardening brought several challenges, many of which Sis has solved. She installed a spigot and hose on the balcony—potted plants dry out quickly, and she knew carrying water from the kitchen every time the plants needed a drink would be a chore. She also had to consider the neighbors below. No one likes a surprise shower, especially when it comes from the neighbor living above

you. Even if the only things underneath your containers are your own toes, getting the water where you want it makes good conservation sense. Sis uses a half-inch hose with a four-foot watering wand on the end—the watering wand lets her reach the hanging baskets and pots tucked away in the corners. The gentle shower of water doesn't dislodge the soil, and saucers under all of the pots help catch drips.

Balconies, like yards, sometimes lack privacy, but planting a hedge or building a fence aren't options for balcony gardeners. The south end of the Kelm's balcony offered a full view of—and from—the condominium complex next door. "Neither Erwin or I had ever lived in an apartment, and I realized when I came out here that everybody could look right smack at me in the summer," Sis said.

She installed a wrought-iron trellis at the south end of the balcony. Morning glories trail up the trellis every summer and moss-lined baskets hang from it. By early July, the neighboring condominium complex disappears behind the vines and flowers. A wooden lattice

This custom-built trellis creates a "living" screen. (Emerson)

or a trellis in a large pot would also work to screen an undesirable view. Potted tropical trees, such as a weeping fig, might be another good choice.

Pots, soil, and water are not lighter than air—their combined weight is sometimes a consideration for container gardeners. The Kelm's balcony is structurally sound, allowing Sis to use any type of pot or soil mix she desires.

She continues to experiment to find the best mix of containers that are durable, offer good drainage, and are large enough not to need constant watering. Her largest planters are four feet long, one foot wide, and 20 inches deep. Made of

wood and lined with galvanized steel, they have drainage holes cut in the bottom and short legs to keep them up off the balcony surface. The galvanized lining keeps the moist soil from coming into contact with the wood, helping to keep the painted wood from rotting and peeling. Sometimes Sis uses planters to hold several individually potted annuals instead of filling the planters with dirt and planting directly into them. She found that geraniums, for example, seem to prefer their own pots, but she likes the look of them massed in the larger planters.

Clay pots are Sis's container of choice. As she puts it: "It isn't natural for plants to be in plastic pots. When they're in the ground, the roots have air. And a plastic pot, particularly if it's in the sun, is going to get even hotter than a clay pot. Clay pots don't dry out as fast. Plus, I don't like the look of plastic."

For hanging baskets, Sis prefers wire forms lined with moss or coconut husks, a new idea she is trying. She noticed that soil sifted down through the sheet moss, so she picked up some coconut husks in Florida and carved them to fit the wire baskets. (These are the outer husks, not the inside nut we see at local grocery stores.) So far she prefers them to the moss— they're attractive and have worked just as well.

To cut down on watering, Sis lines the inside of the sheet moss or the coconut husk with plastic that has holes for drainage. The moss or coconut makes for a natural, woodsy look and makes the containers seem more like part of the garden instead of plastic invaders. Sis also uses wrought-iron containers lined with moss and filled with flowers.

For a really lush container garden, a regular fertilizer program is essential. "The first year I fertilized maybe once a month, or once every six weeks, the way you would in a regular garden," Sis said, "and the things just didn't do too well. I have now come to the conclusion that it's best to fertilize once a week." She uses a 10-30-20 mix: 10 percent nitrogen, 30 percent phosphorous, and 20 percent potassium. She uses a hose-end mixer to save time and fertilizes as she waters.

As to frequency of watering, Sis finds it varies with the pot and the plant. Her large planters only need water three times a week, but smaller containers need daily watering. Tomatoes and hibiscus have been heavy drinkers. The hanging, moss-lined baskets also need a lot of water, especially some half-baskets that she is gradually replacing with larger, full baskets that will need less frequent watering.

The exposure on Sis's balcony is

This high-rise garden makes use of the available space with an array of pots, planter boxes, and hanging baskets. (Emerson)

due east, giving the garden sun from roughly 5:30 a.m. until just before noon. It's enough to grow geraniums, tomatoes, and other sun-lovers, as long as the plants are well-established. Sis also grows a wide variety of herbs, enjoyed for their fragrance as well as for cooking. Planted just outside Sis and Erwin's bedroom, the herbal scents come in with the breeze off the lake.

The Kelm's balcony actually has several separate gardens, much as a yard might have separate garden beds. Off the living room is a private sitting area screened by the morning glories and hanging baskets. The flower colors here are white, shades of blue, and a touch of coral. The garden off the dining room is mostly blue and coral, with a garden table and two chairs that invite you to enjoy the view. The herb garden still has space for flowers. Here the colors are pinks and yellows, which complement the bedroom.

Because the plants and flowers are on display close-up at all times, Sis recommends being tough on nonperformers. "In a small area like this, you've got to keep things looking right. If a clematis isn't looking green and healthy, for example, then forget it. Put something else in." One of the tricks Sis uses is turning the pots regularly so that they flower evenly.

Though appearance is impor-

Beautiful annuals are the result of a regular watering and feeding schedule. (Emerson)

tant, Sis tries to minimize the use of chemicals in her balcony garden. She won't use anything stronger than insecticidal soap. If that doesn't take care of the problem, as in the case of spider mites on marigolds, she just doesn't grow that plant any more.

This attention to planning and detail pays off. "When people come in here and step out on the balcony, they're amazed at the variety of what you can do. They get a warm feeling, like they really are stepping from a house out into a garden."

Condo Gardens

Phillip H. Smith

Living in a townhouse or condominium unit would not, one assumes, provide an opportunity for much typical gardening. People wanting extensive garden space would probably not be attracted to this type of home. From personal experience, however, I have found it is possible both to garden and enjoy the benefits of townhouse living. My townhouse gardens include a deck garden, a vegetable garden, and small perennial border. The search for garden space does involve considerably more ingenuity than it does at a typical single-family home.

Although many residents purchase their units because they wish to avoid the work of maintaining a garden or landscape, they still enjoy the beauty of a well-maintained garden and have absolutely no objection to use of a suitable space by one or more owners who agree to maintain the same. Most complexes have been designed with common architectural features and appearance, and regulations generally prevent altering the exterior appearance of particular units. A resident must expect to be ready with an explanation as to why the garden space will not materially alter the overall appearance or landscape of the complex.

Most townhouse or condo units include some type of deck or patio area, which is an obvious first place for garden use. Quite intensive gardening may be conducted on a deck or patio by use of suitably designed and placed containers. In addition, many townhouse units have a small entry area or dooryard space, which may be densely planted to provide season-long garden enjoyment.

A primary consideration must be the deck or patio exposure. Often a deck will have an exposure suitable only for shade or sun plants, but not both. Plant selection, therefore, becomes quite important. Most disappointments—for both the gardener and the viewer—come from choosing the wrong plants. Annual flowers may make for a colorful and attractive container garden, but only if the plants are selected for the proper exposure and are well-maintained with watering, fertilizer, and periodic pruning.

A variety of containers may be used, including wall-hung flower boxes, hanging pots, and groups of pots or other containers attractively arranged. Many decks have a railing which will support a long flower box. My north-facing front deck has a flower box that is 24 feet long, annually planted with white fibrous begonias and cuttings from a houseplant to provide an attractive combination.

In arranging wall boxes or groups of pots on a deck, think in groups of three or five containers to provide a pleasing arrangement. For height, try a taller corner plant surrounded by lower pots.

With all container plants, watering is crucial. Shaded plants may get along well without watering for quite some time, but containers on a sunny deck may require watering daily, or sometimes even twice a day. There are several schools of thought on container materials, but I prefer plastic pots since they do not dry out so quickly, and the addition of a plastic liner to clay pots is also helpful.

Some gardeners recommend that containers be replenished with new soil each season; I found this unnecessary if a good soil mixture is used initially. In the fall, instead of pulling the plants, merely cut them off at the soil surface with a knife or pruners, and leave the root mass to add texture and organic material to the soil. Then,

in the spring, the container can be dug lightly with a trowel, some fertilizer added, and replanting is easy. Exposed pots or containers should be covered or otherwise protected to prevent frost damage.

For many people, a small deck or patio garden will be enough, but some avid gardeners may want more garden area. For them, there is common ground controlled by a committee of association owners, and this space may be available for garden use by individual owners. The options sometimes include entryways and space directly adjacent to your unit.

Situations will differ, and what may be acceptable at one complex may be objectionable at another. However, a well-maintained garden is a thing of beauty and will likely be so recognized by other residents without objection. Also, a bouquet of fresh flowers or some fresh vegetables provided to neighbors may insure continued use of a garden space for another year.

A gardener contemplating a townhouse or condo style of living may certainly plan on gardening as part of that lifestyle. The sharing of common spaces and common views can be enhanced, rather than abused, by a good gardener.

The following is a list of plants suitable for containers along with their sun requirements.

FLOWER	A—ANNUAL B—BIENNIAL P—PERENNIAL[1] TP—TENDER PERENNIAL[2]	Hanging Basket	Tub or 2 to 5 Gallon Container	Large Container 8-12 Inch Pot	Small Container 4-6 Inch Pot	Full Sun	Partial Shade	Full Shade
Achimenes	TP	•		•	•			•
Ageratum	A			•	•	•	•	
Alyssum	P	•		•				•
Alyssum, Sweet	A	•			•	•	•	
Aster	A			•		•	•	
Balsam	A			•		•	•	
Begonia	TP	•			•		•	•
Browallia	A	•			•	•	•	
Calendula	A			•		•	•	
Candytuft	A or P				•	•	•	
Carnation	A			•		•	•	
Clarkia	A				•	•	•	
Coleus	TP	•			•		•	•
Creeping Zinnia	A	•		•		•		
Daisies (many types)	P			•		•	•	
Dianthus	A or P				•	•	•	
Forget-me-not	B				•	•	•	
Fuchsia	TP	•						•
Gazania	A			•	•	•	•	
Geranium	TP	•	•	•		•	•	
Impatiens	TP	•		•			•	•
Lantana	TP				•	•	•	
Lobelia	A				•	•	•	

FLOWER A—ANNUAL B—BIENNIAL P—PERENNIAL[1] TP—TENDER PERENNIAL[2]		HANGING BASKET	TUB OR 2 TO 5 GALLON CONTAINER	LARGE CONTAINER 8-12 INCH POT	SMALL CONTAINER 4-6 INCH POT	FULL SUN	PARTIAL SHADE	FULL SHADE
Marigold	A			•	•	•	•	
Mignonette	A			•		•	•	
Morning Glory	A	•				•	•	
Nasturtium	A	•				•	•	
Nemesia	A			•		•	•	
Nemophila	A				•	•	•	
Nicotiana	A			•		•	•	
Nierembergia	TP		•	•		•	•	
Pansy	A or P	•			•	•	•	
Petunia	A	•			•	•	•	
Phlox	A or P			•		•	•	
Portulaca	A	•			•	•	•	
Primrose	P			•	•		•	•
Salvia	A			•		•	•	
Schizanthus	A		•	•		•	•	
Snapdragon	A			•		•	•	
Sweet Pea	A	•				•	•	
Thunbergia	A	•				•	•	
Vinca	A	•				•	•	
Zinnia	A		•	•		•	•	

1. Perennials, when grown in containers, need protective covering during the Minnesota winter.
2. In Minnesota, tender perennials must either be grown as annuals or brought indoors (usually into a cool, 30-50°F environment) for the winter.

This listing is courtesy of The National Garden Bureau.

Trellis Gardens
Robert Estelle

For those who garden in containers, trellises and other vertical supports provide many opportunities for growing in places that could not otherwise be used. The greatest advantages are probably to be gained by those who grow fruit or vegetables outdoors, but flowers or vegetables can be grown indoors, in front of windows, by using similar methods.

There can be many advantages in addition to the most obvious one of saving ground space. A second advantage is the decorative effect of displaying a plant as a column or tall specimen or by using it as a screen, rather than having it grow as a low, sprawling mass. Air circulation through and around the plant is improved, eliminating diseases related to excess moisture. Leaves are more uniformly exposed to light. Another benefit can be realized from the reduced danger of soil-borne disease or of damage by animals or insects. The plant may be easier to tend, not only for the able-bodied gardender, but also by those who are disabled or aged.

Up, Down, and Around

There are several distinct types of support systems that help plants grow up, instead of out, depending to some extent on the size and growth habits of the plants. Small plants, such as lettuces or strawberries, are often grown in individual pots or in easily moved planters set on bleacher-like systems of shelves. Also, such plants can be grown in a "plant wall," in which a soil mix or soil substitute is held in place between outer layers of wire netting and plastic sheets. In such a system, the plant roots are inserted into cuts made through the plastic, and the leaves ultimately conceal the wall in which they are growing.

A second type might be called the "cascade" form of planting. This would include any method by which trailing plants are allowed to grow down, naturally and without special support, from a container on top of a column, a stand, or a wall.

One of the most underused ways to reshape container gardening involves using trellises in combination with planting in containers. In most cases, this kind of trellis is considered mainly as a support for the plant, but it can and should also serve as a pattern for the form of the plant.

In fact, consider using trellises not only to support vining plants, but to reshape stiff, upright plants as well. Trellised plants can assume and maintain a shape that will improve their ornamental value or their fruiting capacity.

The Pick of the Crop

All of the above advantages can contribute to much more satisfying results when growing fruits and vegetables in containers. Several that are suitable for growing in containers with the support of a framework include tomatoes, cucumbers, pole beans, melons, and potatoes. Peppers and eggplants are good container vegetables, and, with their often top-heavy crops of fruit and their tall stems, can almost always benefit from the use of a trellis. Peas certainly need a trellis, but are probably not an ideal container crop. The same is true of squash and pumpkins which, because of the size and weight of the vine and fruit, may not be good container subjects. If we do not restrict ourselves to vegetable crops, gourds and flowering ornamental vines are also good subjects for vertical gardening with trellises. Tomatoes, of course, are the almost universal choice for gardeners of all sorts. They are excellent container plants and require support.

Some fruits can be grown in containers and include perennial vines, plants with canes, bushes, or small trees. All of these will benefit not only from proper pruning, but also from some degree of training, support, and protection. Raspberries and blackberries can be tied to a fan, and the frame will facilitate the use of bird-proof netting. Grapevines require support and protection from birds, and they offer endless decorative possibilities, as well as fruitfulness.

Other perennials include roses that trail or climb and are similarly

A trellis system dramatically increases your growing space. (King)

rewarding subjects for containers and trellises. Among other bushy perennials, gooseberries, currants, and blueberries are good subjects for training. Gooseberries and currants can each be pruned to grow on a single trunk, and currants have been grown as espaliers. Dwarfed apple or pear trees can be grown in a variety of traditional or free-form espaliers. Other trees or shrubs, such as cherries, cherry-plums, figs, or citrus can be grown experimentally in containers and should be provided with trellis frameworks for training and to make it easier to protect the fruit.

An Ideal Trellis System

Any trellis system for container-grown fruits or vegetables should meet a number of important requirements. Above all, it should give adequate support to the plant and to the crop. The use of a single stick, pushed into the soil through the roots of the plant, is next to useless and a law should be enacted against the practice!

The support device should be effective, inexpensive, simple, and easy to maintain. It is especially important that the support structure be easy to store when not in use. Also, it should adapt to any standard nursery pot and to most other containers.

The whole thing—pot, plant and trellis—should be easy to move as a single unit without disturbing the plant and its fruit. It should also be stable and sturdy. The trellis should be unobtrusive (invisible, if possible), hidden, as much as possible, by the plant. The ideal support structure should be adaptable to a variety of plants, perennial or annual, so that a single design will serve for several different fruits and vegetables.

A number of very important functions can be performed by a trellis, in addition to supporting the plant. The trellis should make it possible to support protective covers against frost, wind, and hail, or hard rain. It should allow the gardener to hang a covering of netting to protect against birds or animals. The trellis should also allow the use of fabric or other materials to shade the plant and the pot from direct sun. These protective functions of the trellis may be almost as valuable as its ability to support the plant.

The most successful structures take one of two basic forms, that of a tripod or that of an A-frame. Another useful trellis, the rectangular frame with a grid of horizontal strips, can be set into the ground behind the container or attached to a wall. This type of trellis, while certainly adaptable to container gardening, restricts the gardener's choice of location and reduces the portability of the plant and container.

Raised-Bed Gardening

Bobbi Smidt Johnson

I f you're short on growing space or want to add another dimension to your existing garden, consider raised beds—a way of getting the best of both container and traditional gardening. My husband, Cavour, and I became advocates of raised-bed gardening when faced with a narrow city lot that needed more character and definition. Besides displaying a variety of plant colors and textures, the beds served as a natural border along a sidewalk shared with a neighbor and at the back of our property where a fence was not an option.

Some years later, when we moved to the country, I looked forward to the supposedly unlimited space that would exist for our gardens. As it turned out, our sunniest space was an overgrown field of sumac, blackberry bushes, ostrich ferns, and wood ticks. It was also 150 yards from the house and the nearest water source. Two other sunny, closer-to-home options remained: one was the sprawling area directly in front of our garage, also known, unfortunately, as the driveway; the other was a steep embankment of sand, which we had tentatively labeled our back yard.

We had no real choice. Back yard it was, and the digging began. We had just enough level ground to build two raised beds the first year—enough to hold tomatoes, radishes, spinach, carrots, and a few peppers. But we wanted more garden. More garden meant less embankment. How were we going to handle this gardening challenge? The answer came quickly. More raised beds, this time terraced into the hillside.

We devised a five-year plan to carry out our design. Each year we headed up the hill a little more with a new phase of beds. Though we were eager to have the space available all at once, carrying out the plan over five summers was rewarding for several reasons:

- One, we set reasonable construction goals we could implement and finish by planting time.
- Two, construction costs were spread out.
- Three, having a season to try out each new phase allowed us to make alterations to the remain-

ing master plan.

Cavour did the major designing, building, and dirty work, with a few token loads of dirt hauled by me. My specialty is the planting (with the exception of the beets) and maintenance of the beds. We both learned a lot in the process.

Planning and Construction

Once you have selected the site for your raised-bed garden, you are ready to decide on the finished size, organize the basic tools, and make a materials list. Most raised beds are built using landscape timbers, and since most landscape timbers come in 8-foot lengths, think in 2, 4, 8, 12, and 16-foot sizes.

When you're picking out the timbers at your local lumber yard, look for straight, solid pieces. A warped timber is practically impossible to incorporate into a long, level layer. If you do end up with one by mistake, cut it up to use in sections for a small bed.

Don't forget to include walkways and steps in your garden. You'll want easy access around each bed for planting, weeding, harvesting, and general maintenance. Options for walkways include recessed patio blocks, bricks, treated planks, or crushed rock; on level ground, where rain won't wash it away, decorative bark looks nice, too.

If you're building raised beds on what is now lawn, use a spade to dig out the rough dimensions. Remove the grass in chunks if possible, with a couple inches of soil intact, and use them to repair problem spots in your yard.

If the construction site is dirt or sand, just lay out the timbers marking the sides of the bed. Gradually dig out or build up the area underneath the timbers until they are level. Adding a one-inch layer of sand beneath each timber allows for easier leveling. Make sure the base timbers are snug-fitting at each corner to hold in the dirt. There is no need to toenail the corners; the nailed upper layers will hold everything in place.

Next, add layers much as you would stack Lincoln logs, interlocking the corners, until you reach the desired garden height. Keep in mind that tall beds need many wheelbarrows of dirt. Secure the timbers to the layer below with 12-inch spikes, double-checking to see that the pounding has not disturbed the levelness of the bed. When possible, place the side of the top timber with the most knots facing down, since knots tend to seep pitch in warm weather.

If the beds are terraced into a hillside, the steepness of the hill and the size of the bed determine the depth. A steep hill can be very costly if timbers are used for all four sides, especially on the uphill

Raised beds provide a gardener with "weeding benches" as well as new design opportunities. (Johnson)

side where much of the garden wall is underground. When we built the second tier of beds, we used the grade of the hill as part of the container. The timbers visible on the back edge of each hillside bed were placed on top of an earth wall formed by the slope. Besides saving on materials, it saved having to do a lot of excavating and refilling later.

As we headed up the incline, we always tried to use the framing of the lower unit as a base for the next uphill segment. This, too, saved on materials as well as giving us a level platform upon which to build. We also found that recessing the walkways was more visually appealing than building them flush with the top edge of the lower bed.

Learn As You Go

At the beginning of the third year, we modified our plans. In looking at our three tiers of raised beds, we could see that some variation was needed to break the monotony of layer upon layer of landscape timbers. We also noticed that the hill was getting steeper. As a solution, we decided to place the timbers upright and use them as corner posts in the raised beds; at least half of each post was needed below the original ground level for strength. Between the corner posts, we used 2x12-inch pressure-treated planking for the walls of the beds, which we fastened to the posts with nails. This resulted in a faster way to meet the grade of the slope and introduced a new look to the project. It also involved fewer materials and less excavation. Because of the steeper grade, the beds still required a lot of black dirt to fill them up, however.

If we were building this design today, we'd be sure to install the boards inside the posts and we would use wood screws instead of nails, because the weight of the soil against the boards we nailed on the outside has started to force them away from the posts.

There are a few other things we learned along the way:

- When we doubled the rise of a step at the steep part of the hill, we did it to avoid digging out part of the bank to create the room for two smaller steps. It was a shortcut that shouldn't have been taken. It's an unnaturally long drop compared to the one-timber height our feet are used to on all the other steps.

- Where we have an upper and lower bed directly connected to each other without a walkway, I am always tempted to walk on the ledge common to both to get at the center of the lower bed. Some day my tightrope luck will run out and I'll take a two-foot plunge, which won't hurt me, but could pulverize quite a few healthy plants

below. If you want to avoid this, place walkways between every bed or keep each connected bed narrow enough to reach the center from three directions. A simple solution is to install a six-inch board across the back of the bottom bed to create a maintenance walkway.

Garden Maintenance

Taking care of raised-bed gardens is no more work—often less—than traditional gardens. Each spring we spade in peat moss and compost, and sometimes a little more sand if it seems necessary to get faster drainage. Invariably, some of the beds settle over the winter, so we supplement those with more black dirt as well. Other than that, there's very little to do before getting in our first spring crops.

In the fall, we clean out the beds, but do not cover the timbers. We have not had to mulch our perennials, but give extra care to those with sensitive root structures. Harsher winter conditions may occur in raised beds, so provide extra protection or plant them in the beds closer to ground level.

Growing Vegetables in Containers

Robert Estelle

Normally we think of vegetables being grown in the ground, in the sort of gardens traditionally found in rural or suburban back yards. But fewer people every year have access to such a space. Also, a great number of vegetable gardens have always been unsuitable for growing food plants because of poor soil, lack of sun, competition from roots of shrubs and trees, inadequate protection from frost and wind. Renting a garden plot is often inconvenient. Growing vegetables in containers offers an interesting alternative.

Container gardeners are always being asked about the advantages and disadvantages to container growing, compared to traditional growing in the open ground. Here are my top 15 reasons for using containers:

(1) Soil texture, sanitation, and nutrient content can be better controlled and altered than in the open ground. (2) Small areas of ground or sunlight, paved areas, or space on structures can be used. (3) Root competition from trees and shrubs is avoided. (4) Plants can be seen better, since they are elevated by the pot, permitting better observation, culture, and aesthetic appreciation. (5) Plants can be placed in more accessible locations for elderly or disabled gardeners. (6) Experimental changes of location, for cultural or aesthetic advantage, are always possible. (7) No part of the lawn or permanent landscaping needs to be altered or destroyed in order to make a vegetable garden. (8) Plants can easily be given to others as gifts. (9) Creative design and fabrication of containers, plant supports, and display structures are encouraged. (10) Plants can be incorporated into sitting or living areas, where they can be viewed and enjoyed, rather than being relegated to a separate area away from the house. (11) The area around the plants is less likely to be rough, irregular, dirty, or muddy. (12) Insect control is usually easier where plants are slightly above ground level. (13) Plants can be moved into sheltered areas in the fall, if they are still bearing when frosts come. (14) Weeding is easier. (15) Water is more likely to go directly to the root area of container plants than

in most open-ground irrigation, resulting in better growth and conservation practices.

Obviously, there are a few drawbacks, such as costs of pots, more frequent watering, limited root growth and soil volume, learning what varieties will do best, and developing special skills to succeed in a new type of gardening. While each of these disadvantages may be fundamental and weighty considerations, one who gardens in containers is liable to become an advocate.

One past year's garden—all in pots—attracted some attention among the neighbors. In future years, we tried to be more systematic, but enthusiasm often outruns our scientific detachment. We did, however, attempt to record our progress.

Seeding Plants for this container gardening project were started in the usual ways. Plants needing an early start were seeded in small containers and grown briefly under lights in a basement light-garden area. As soon as possible, to avoid legginess, the seedling containers were moved to an unheated, lean-to greenhouse. When the danger of frost was past, they were transplanted to intermediate-size pots or to their final growing container and placed outside or, in a few cases, into a cold frame. Plants not requiring this early planting and transplanting procedure were seeded directly into the containers in which they were to grow to maturity.

The seeds were bought in February, by mail, from two major seed companies. Buying in this way allows the usual prolonged, delightful consideration of every plant and every variety during the long, dark hours of winter and curbs the unconsidered haste of the impulse buyer. The seeding followed this schedule: cabbage and lettuce, mid-March; peppers and tomatoes, early-April; squash, early-April; and cucumbers, musk melons, and watermelon, mid-April.

The transplanting and removal to the outdoors took place in mid-May, cautiously and with only a few pots at first, when it seemed that the weather was settling into a no-frost pattern.

Vegetables Selected The vegetables chosen were selected, in part, out of audacity rather than from reasonable conservatism. There are a number of unspectacular, reliable plants, well-adapted to containers, which could have been chosen. But a large number of vine vegetables were selected in order to experiment with supports and trellises. The vine vegetables chosen included pole beans, tomatoes, cucumbers, squash, and melons. The only major vining vegetable that was omitted was the potato. Potatoes were grown successfully in containers last year, but the yield seemed not to justify the space. That, however, is a matter of opinion only.

Containers An unlimited range of containers and their many accessories—elevated stands, hanging basket slings, cache-pots and decorative insulating skirts, wind screens, sun reflectors and covers— are available. The container itself, of course, is the basic element, and must be stable, durable, well-drained, and large enough to contain the roots and the necessary nutrients and moisture for the plant. It should be attractive (or capable of being hidden or embellished), and it is advantageous if it can be moved without too much difficulty.

These large planter boxes are a great choice for small-space vegetable gardening (Brusic)

The most common container is the plastic pot, available in all practical sizes and in a variety of shapes. It is cheaper, more durable, easier to clean, and more easily available than the clay pot and probably more useful to the home vegetable gardener, although not considered as attractive by many. For the vegetable gardener, the most useful sizes are 6, 9, and 12-inch sizes. These pots can last up to ten years in use. They can generally be stored, nested, in a relatively small space when empty. A thin, nonporous, smooth, not-too-rigid plastic should be chosen.

Plastic or sheet metal pots will heat the soil mass when the sun shines on them. This is an advantage in early spring (or, perhaps, in fall), but a disadvantage in midsummer. Plastic pots need shielding from the sun. The wooden tub or trough combines shield and container into one unit, insulating as well as maintaining the earth mass and its moisture. Wooden containers are generally more expensive and less durable than plastic nursery pots, but open up a vast field for design of special shapes, finishes, colors, and ornamentation.

THE NORTHERN GARDENER'S LIBRARY

Chapter 2

Tips and Techniques

Basics of Container Watering

Soil Mixes for Containers

Building a Planter Box

Roses in Raised Beds

Starting Seeds Indoors

Growing Alpines in Containers

Basics of Container Watering

Robert Estelle

Plants all need water in order to live, but improper watering is probably the single greatest cause of damage to plants, particularly those growing in containers. Damage is more often due to excessive watering and water retention than to lack of water. It is not just a matter of too much or too little. The temperature of the water, the manner in which it is applied, and substances in the water all affect plant health. Watering also depends on the composition and texture of the soil, the type of container, the location of the plant, as well as idiosyncrasies of both the plant and the gardener. The proper management of water depends not so much on supplying it on a fixed schedule, as on regularly observing a whole network of good gardening practices.

Container Size

Successful watering begins with selecting a container of proper size. The larger the plant and the more vigorous its growth, the more moisture it will lose through its leaves. A plant the size of a mature lettuce, for instance, if it is grown in a pot less than six inches in diameter and six inches in height, will probably wilt within a day after a thorough watering. Although it is sometimes advised that plants not be put into too large a pot, if the plant's need for water is the only consideration and the soil is well drained, no pot can be too large. Other matters, such as appearance, weight, and cost may dictate the use of a smaller pot.

Container Type

Conventional containers include those made of plastic, clay, wood, paper, or other materials. Porous containers dry out more quickly. Because potting mixtures are sometimes poorly aerated, porous pots are often advocated. I prefer non-porous pots and a well-drained soil.

Water loss can be reduced if the pot has a reflective outer surface, or if it is placed behind or within a shield. Mulching the top of the soil may also help. Cache pots—decorative, undrained pots into which the container holding the soil is set—can serve as sun shields, but need to be drained periodically, so

Your potted plants can look as healthy as these if you choose the right size containers and take the time to water properly. (Reid)

they don't collect water and injure the roots within the inner pot.

Container Shape

The shape of the container also influences the water-holding capacity of the soil. A tall container will have a longer capillary column than a shallow one, and will drain better. A shallow container, such as a wooden flat, will have more surface area for the same volume of soil, and the top of the soil may dry out quickly unless mulched. Odd-shaped containers—such as ceramic figurines with holes for planting—may collect undrained water in some places, causing roots to decay. Some ornamental planters may have no drainage holes at all and, despite the usually recommended layers of crushed rock at the bottom of the container, the roots will be killed by the stagnant water that will collect. Drainage holes should be located on the sides of the container, so that placing the pot on a flat surface will not close them, or the pot should be raised to allow drainage if the holes are in the bottom.

I recommend more frequent use of planters which can hold several plants. The plants can all share the same soil and moisture, reducing fluctuations in water supply. Even if you don't plant directly in the planter, it can serve as an attractive sun-shield, holding several individually potted plants.

Container Location

Sunny, hot sites will overheat the soil and increase moisture loss from the plant's leaves. Exposure to wind will also increase water loss. One should not place a container directly onto a paved surface exposed to the hot sun, nor leave the plant untended in an enclosed space such as a greenhouse, cold frame, or porch, where temperatures can become extremely high. On the other hand, dark, chilly, airless locations can aggravate the soggy condition of a soil that is not well drained.

Most plants appreciate a cool, sheltered location. (MSHS).

Watering Method

Properly designed watering cans are probably the best means of supplying water to potted plants. They can, however, be very heavy and they do require methodical attention to every plant. Most watering cans are not of good design, and it is worth the trouble and money to locate one of the excellent British types, for sale by some importers of garden tools. A garden hose with the usual nozzle will leave the plant bruised and broken by the force of the chilling stream of water. Watering wands and nozzles specially designed to reduce the force of the water are certainly an improvement. But if you have the time and patience, there is nothing better than room-temperature water from a well-designed watering can.

The average container gardener may be able to adapt commercial methods for use on a smaller scale. These include permanent overhead sprinklers and spray systems. They may be costly to install, and need careful regulation to prevent excessive watering or waste. They also may chill the plants if water is used directly from city water mains. Mist systems are normally designed for rooting cuttings or for increasing the humidity around tropical plants and do not supply adequate moisture for mature plants.

Drip or trickle systems provide

continuous watering through small tubes, one for each pot, connected to a central feeder pipe. Such systems are best where all plants are of similar culture, a uniform size, in pots of the same type, growing in the same soil mix, and relatively close together—a situation often found in a commercial greenhouse but seldom in a gardener's backyard.

Individual Styles

The worst possible pattern is one that includes impulsive, overprotective, nervous, and continual watering. Gardeners who display this syndrome think of their plants as thirsty, sensitive creatures who must continually be refreshed with large quantities of cool water. Such people may, unintentionally, kill more plants than do the opposite type, the negligent gardener.

Be willing to allow the soil to dry out (but not excessively) and then soak each pot gently and thoroughly with water the same temperature as the air. Allowing the water to sit in order to warm it has the added benefit of reducing chemical content, such as chlorine, which might be harmful to the plants. In addition, avoid home-softened water or water from sources that contain biological or chemical contaminants; check with the county extension office if in doubt.

How Much is Enough?

Everyone who grows plants in containers will have to develop the ability to determine the amount of water remaining in the soil and to evaluate the moisture-holding capacity of a soil mix. Poke a finger an inch or more into the soil in order to feel its moisture. This is a bit messy, and not fully accurate, but it's a good guide.

If you're serious about finding the real truth, you might carefully unpot and repot small plants occasionally to monitor them. Soggy soil and dark, decayed roots or, conversely, a completely dry soil mass are not reassuring signs. For those less inclined to detective work, observing the above ground portion of the plant may be sufficient. Wilting, dropping leaves, and drying foliage are signs of stress due to lack of moisture. Yellowed leaves and attacks of aphids may well be signs of excessive water.

So, for healthy and beautiful plants, make sure you are using the right type and size of container, put it in the right location, and take time to water properly. Your plants will respond to the added attention.

Soil Mixes for Containers:

A Matter of Three Opinions

Charlie King

The successful use of retaining walls, window boxes, and other types of containers is often a key element in creating a beautiful garden. Success with container gardening starts with the soil mixture, which must provide adequate drainage. An effective soil mix for containers should consist of three parts commercial potting soil, two parts well-decayed compost or peat moss, and one part perlite or coarse sand. A measuring cup of 0-20-20 fertilizer per bushel of soil, well blended in, would be a good starting point.

Container soil must be porous and should not pack. It should hold water like a sponge but allow excess water to drain quickly. During the growing season, annuals grown in containers respond favorably to water-soluble fertilizer. Keep in mind that all container-grown plants will require much more water than the same plants grown in an open garden; consequently, there will be considerably more leaching away of plant nutrients. Therefore fertilizer should be provided every seven to ten days.

Fish emulsion is an excellent water soluble fertilizer, and there are many fine commercial types. One that is low in nitrogen will work best for container plants.

Sis Kelm

Soil is just as important in container gardening as it is in traditional gardening. The advantage is that you can custom mix the soil. After balcony gardening for eight years, Sis has definite opinions on soil mixes. "I find potting soil very difficult to work with. I prefer just plain old dirt with good drainage. If it's too heavy, then add your own peat or whatever you need to lighten it. And the potting soil with the perlite is for the birds. You end up with that perlite all up at the top and it blows all over."

She doesn't completely replace the soil in her containers each year, but simply adds to it as needed. One year Sis tried adding earthworms to the large planters boxes to improve the soil. "I put a hundred worms in each box. I pulled about a thousand worms out. I don't know if it made any difference, but it didn't do any harm.

Only a couple crawled out during the summer."

Robert Estelle

The type of soil mix is of utmost importance in maintaining an adequate supply of water without depriving roots of necessary air.

In the 1930s the British John Innes Institute devised a loam made from manure and pasture turf, to which were added sand, peat moss, limestone, and fertilizing substances. Later formulations for potting mixes depended on chemical nutrients, added to relatively inert artificial soils. The University of California mix prescribes sand and milled sphagnum moss, and the later Cornell University lightweight mixes used commercially produced mineral products, such as vermiculite, mixed with milled sphagnum. The advantages of these sterile mixes are their freedom from pathogens and their ability to hold water and air. The disadvantages are their increasing cost and the gardener's forced dependence on commercial sources of supply.

Suffice it to say that ordinary garden soil will not work very well in containers. Potting soil needs at least some amendment, some artificiality in order to properly provide air, water, and nutrients to container-grown plants.

These geraniums are off to a great start in a soil mix blended to hold water yet allow for drainage. (MSHS)

Building a Planter Box

Robert Estelle

Many vegetables, herbs, and ornamental plants can be grown successfully in six-inch pots. Gardeners often prefer containers of this size, since they weigh very little, require only a limited amount of soil, and are easily emptied, washed, and stored at the end of the season.

Larger containers have at least one great advantage, however; they are definitely visible and can be desirable objects in the landscape. Small pots tend to disappear, to be overlooked, or seem insignificant on a patio or against a building. They are more likely to dry out in hot sun and be tipped over by wind or animals.

Window boxes were once as common as front porches. They are no longer as often built and used, because of their heavy weight when filled, the difficulty of maintaining a continuing succession of attractive plants, and the difficulty of removing and replacing the soil. Building a lightweight planter box, to be filled with plants grown in individual pots, eliminates most of the problems associated with the traditional window box, at the same time preserving its advantages and even providing additional benefits.

The planter box has the advantage of mobility. It can be set wherever its length fits the space. Several can be placed end to end, to define and emphasize a longer line. Planters can be set on a balcony or porch, at the edge of the floor, or on a wide railing. A patio offers all kinds of possibilities, including the center of the picnic table. Fences and walls can be made less severe and more decorative by using planter boxes. The edges of walks or paved areas can be lined with plants.

And there is always the option of setting a planter on brackets, attached to the wall of a house beneath a window, as the traditional window box was placed. Because planter boxes are easily moved and because there are so many possible locations, endless experiment is possible. Early in the season it can even serve, with panes of glass across its top, as a cold frame to protect seedlings started indoors.

Build it Yourself

An efficient and attractive planter can be built with a minimum of material and very little labor. The box can be made in any size, but the one described here was designed to hold five six-inch pots. This results in a convenient three-foot length, neither too small to be visually attractive nor too large to be lifted, even when filled with plants. The space inside the planter allows room at the sides of the pots and between them, permitting foliage to spread and air to circulate. Here's what you'll need:

2 pieces lap siding, 8 inches wide (actual width 7-1/2 inches), each 3 feet long, for sides.

1 piece of lumber, 6 inches wide (actual width 5-1/2 inches), 3/4-inch thick, 3 feet long, for bottom.

2 pieces lumber or plywood, 6-3/4 inches wide, 3/4-inch thick, each 6-3/4 inches long, for ends.

2 pieces lumber or plywood, 3/4-inch wide, 3/4-inch thick, each 6-3/4 inches long, for feet.

12 galvanized nails; common, fourpenny size (1-1/2 inches long), for attaching sides.

10 galvanized nails; common, eightpenny size (2-1/2 inches long), for attaching bottom and feet.

Once the pieces are cut to size, assembly is very easy. The drawing makes clear most of the details of construction. Begin by nailing the bottom to the two ends. If you own a small drill, you may wish to drill pilot holes—thinner than the nail and not as deep—to avoid splitting the wood when nails are driven in.

The bottom is not as wide as the end-pieces and should be nailed, using the longer, 2-1/2 inch nails (three at each end), so that the end pieces extend 5/8-inch on either side of the bottom. This means that there will be a space, 5/8-inch wide, on both sides of the bottom, the full length of the planter. The sides (of eight-inch drop siding) will not touch the piece of wood which forms the bottom, and cannot be nailed to it. The sides are nailed only to the ends of the box. These spaces between the sides and the bottom allow drainage and ventilation.

After the bottom is fastened, the sides should be attached with the thick edge of the siding flush with the top of the end pieces. Twelve of the shorter, 1-1/2 inch nails should be used, three at each end of each side. The box is now complete except for the two feet, which should be nailed about 3/4-inch in from each end of the bottom and extending evenly on either side of it. Use two of the longer, 2-1/2 inch nails for attaching each of the feet. These will keep the bottom of the planter from resting directly on wet pavement or soil, reducing

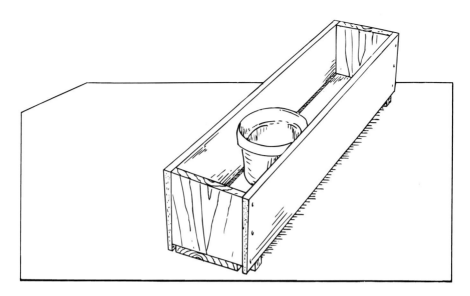

Planter-boxes can be used in a variety of situations. A small herb garden near your kitchen might be a good first choice.

decay. It will be easier to replace the feet than the bottom, if dampness causes deterioration.

Planter boxes can be built in any size to hold any number of pots, large or small. Unless the gardener has very definite plans to fill a particular space with plants of a certain kind, the planter described here should allow plenty of experiment.

Use the planter for vegetables that can be grown well in six-inch pots, such as lettuce and other salad greens, small tomatoes, and smaller root vegetables, such as radishes, little carrots and turnips, beets, and bunching onions. Alpine strawberries are another good choice. Herbs that grow well in six-inch pots include some of the most popular, such as parsley, chives, basil, mint, sage, fragrant geraniums, nasturtiums, and others. Ornamental plants suitable for pots of six-inch diameter include some variety of almost every popular garden plant. The range is both exciting and bewildering—whether one plants to enjoy color, fragrance, flavor, or nutrition, there is no lack of suitable plants to fill the adventurous gardener's planter box. In fact, the gardener may have to become a carpenter to keep up with the demand.

Gardening Skill

Techniques for Successful Container Gardening

1. Start with the right soil mix. Container soil must be porous. It should hold water like a sponge, yet allow water to drain. Ordinary garden soil generally doesn't work. A good basic recipe is as follows:

   2 parts potting soil, garden soil, or compost
   1 part sand, vermiculite, or perlite to lighten the soil
   1 part spagnum moss or leaf mold (for vegetables, use only 1/4 in mixture)

   Be sure to mix and moisten soil before planting (let stand overnight after mixing and watering with warm water).

2. Provide proper drainage. If your pots have large holes in bottom, try putting down a layer of old pantyhose. If you have some decorative containers that don't have drainage holes, put down at least 1" of pea gravel, broken pot chips, or styrofoam packing peanuts.

3. Use a large enough pot. The larger the plant and the more vigorous its growth, the more moisture it will lose through its leaves. You don't want to have to water twice a day.

4. Pick suitable locations. Try to shelter your containers from the wind. Keep them out of hot, sunny sites, especially paved areas.

5. Keep your plants cool. A layer of mulch can help retain moisture and keep containers cooler. Use bark, gravel, or moss. If you want to provide more insulation, choose a large container of any kind. Then select a plain pot that is 2-3" smaller in diameter. Set the smaller pot into the larger pot and fill the space between the pots with spagnum moss, sheet moss, or mulched bark.

6. Fertilize. Fertilizer is going to leach out of your container soil faster than in your garden. Use a water-soluble fertilizer and follow the label instructions.

Roses in Raised Beds

Robert Mugaas

Each spring a rose gardener's thoughts often turn to finding some new places to squeeze in a few more plants. Finding these new garden spots may be easier said than done, however. Even if you can find an area in full sun, the soil may be in very poor condition. One solution to some of the more difficult soil problems is to build a raised bed to grow your roses in. Much of the rose growing I have done has involved raised beds, and they have helped solve a number of difficult soil problems which I have encountered.

A raised bed is nothing more than a planting bed elevated over the existing soil. Raised beds allow the gardener to build a much higher quality root zone than that afforded by the existing soil. Raising the soil level over the existing grade usually results in better soil drainage. Also, the raised bed area will usually dry out faster, resulting in warmer soils in spring.

Once you have chosen a location, the next decision will be the size and shape of the raised bed. While the term raised bed has been used extensively with respect to vegetable gardening, usually meaning square or rectangle shapes, it is usually much more interesting to design an area for roses which is not an exact square or rectangle.

If you like to walk around your rose beds and be able to do maintenance without tromping on the soil, make the planting area no wider than four to five feet. This

Potted roses wait to be planted into the rich soil of this raised bed. (MSHS)

will easily accommodate two rows of roses which will be reachable from either side of the bed. Larger, wider beds will accommodate different planting schemes and facilitate walking in and around the bushes, both for maintenance and for viewing. However, construction of large beds will require more materials and may be more of a project than you want to take on.

Raised rose beds can be constructed with or without side supports. The advantage of using supports is that the soil is held uniformly around the plants, minimizing the amount of soil erosion from the sides of the raised beds. Some people also like the neater appearance of an enclosed structure. I've even seen raised beds with brick mower strips around the timbers to keep the sides of the beds neat and tidy. Although I prefer the look of a raised bed with side supports, I have found little difference in performance using either style.

Side supports can be made from treated landscape timbers, either four by fours or three by fives. If elevations of one to two feet or more will be needed, such as on a hillside, larger timbers may be needed and proper anchoring techniques are required to hold the timbers in the hillside and keep the bank from collapsing. This kind of construction may require the aid of a professional landscaper.

I have also tried using both one-and two-inch boards, but they have warped, even when they were nailed onto stakes driven securely into the ground. The amount of warping was enough to make the beds unattractive after less than one growing season.

Be sure to choose landscape timbers which are safe for use around plants. Timbers which have been treated with copper naphthanate or chromated copper arsenate (CCA) are suitable. They are available in green or brown. Be sure the timbers have been pressure treated to get the maximum penetration of preservative into the wood. Painting the preservative on the outside of the timber is not nearly as effective or as long-lasting as pressure treatment.

Avoid timbers which have been treated with pentachlorophenol (penta) or creosote. These chemicals will volatilize from recently treated timbers, harming plants. While these timbers may be fine for other parts of a landscape plan, they should not be used where they will be in direct proximity to plants, especially roses. I have seen situations where roses have been destroyed by the vapors emanating from these types of timbers.

Stonework and several of the new types of masonry block can also be used to create raised beds. These materials are not as confining in terms of design as are the long, straight landscape timbers.

These handsome roses are flourishing in this backyard raised bed. Stonework and interlocking masonry block are other choices for framing. (MSHS)

Also, depending on the materials used in the rest of the landscape, stone may be more appropriate than wood.

While exact heights for raised beds are a matter of personal choice, there are a couple of rules of thumb that can be used to determine an approximate height. If the existing soil is very poor, such as a heavy, poorly drained soil or a coarse, gravelly soil, a minimum depth of 8 to 12 inches will be necessary. Where soil conditions are not as extreme, a height of 4 to 8 inches will be adequate.

Once the size and shape of the raised bed has been determined, you can approximate the amount of soil needed to fill the area by determining the cubic feet. To do this, multiply the bed length by the width and the height and divide this number by 27 (the number of cubic feet in a cubic yard). For example, a 4-foot wide by 10-foot long by 6-inch high raised bed has a volume of approximately three-quarters of a cubic yard. This will help you when you go to buy topsoil, organic material, mulches, etc., as this is how nurseries sell these supplies.

Begin preparing the area for the raised bed by breaking up the soil surface. If grass is growing where the bed will be, thoroughly break up the sod with a shovel or tiller before adding anything. I have not found it necessary to kill the grass before working it back into the soil, as is often recommended. A thorough job of breaking up the sod is sufficient to destroy most of the grass and prevent it from coming back into the bed. Besides, this addition of organic matter will only improve the soil.

Once the soil surface has been prepared, the next step is to add whatever amendments or additional soil are needed to raise the bed to the desired height. In addition to topsoil, finished or nearly finished compost, peat moss, and other decomposed organic material make wonderful additions to any new rose bed. I have often created the height needed in the raised bed by only adding these types of soil amendments. The end result is a rich, well-drained, easy-to-manage soil which has grown many beautiful rose plants and flowers.

If topsoil is going to be added, select one with a loam or sandy loam texture. Adding heavy, poor quality soil will only make your problem worse. Request that the soil be pulverized prior to delivery to eliminate having to work with large soil clumps. If you have the opportunity to see a representative soil test of the material before you purchase it, you will be able to avoid purchasing topsoil which may be too alkaline or too acidic.

Whatever materials you choose to work with, begin by working some of it into the existing soil to create a more even root zone, thus avoiding the problems associated with soil layering. Also, be sure to mix together the various amendments and any topsoil as you add them to the raised-bed area. The use of a tiller will make this job easier and faster, as well as ensure you end up with a uniform distribution of these materials throughout the raised bed.

The finished soil level should be slightly higher than the side supports or the desired height of the unsupported raised bed to allow for settling. Thoroughly water the entire raised bed and allow the materials to settle for a week or two before planting. Better still, build the bed in fall and allow it to settle over winter. In spring, any additional soil can be added as the bed is prepared for planting.

If the raised bed does not have side supports, simply rake the soil from around the edges into the middle of the bed. Using a shovel, make a clean edge around the bed, raking the soil away from the edge into the bed. This will help keep weeds from growing into the bed and give it a neater appearance. Six-inch plastic landscape edging can be used to accomplish the same thing.

After all of the necessary soil preparations are completed, the beds are ready for planting. Where raised beds are unsupported, roses should be planted more towards the middle of the bed. The edge areas will be sloped downward and it will be harder to thoroughly water and fertilize plants near the edges, as the tendency will be for water to run off. This problem can be partially alleviated by using a heavy mulch on these edge areas. A soaker hose, which can be placed on the soil surface and covered with a mulch, can also partially remedy this problem, as the slowly released water has a much greater chance to infiltrate the soil before running off. An organic mulch along the edges will also help buffer the greater extremes in temperatures which the edge areas are subject to.

The edge effect is also present when side supports are used, but it is not quite as exteme. Since supported raised beds have only the flat, upper surface exposed, water and water/fertilizer solutions are much less prone to run off. However, as the timbers weather and settle, cracks can develop between them, providing areas for water to escape. And, as with unsupported raised beds, the area of greatest soil environmental variation will be along the perimeter, making organic mulches a good practice with side-supported raised beds also.

Winter protection of roses growing in raised beds is not particularly different than where they are growing in ground beds. Once the roses have been cut back and mounded or buried with the Minnesota tip method, protective mulches can be applied over the top of the bed. Covering hay, bags of leaves, or other types of winter cover should be placed over the top of the beds and along sides where side supports have not been used. Where side supports have been used, it is better to bank a good supply of mulch up against the sides. This will help minimize temperature extremes along the edges of the rose bed. However, this can create a problem where grass or other garden plants are growing up to the raised bed, as heavy mulches may result in dead areas of grass the next spring.

I have seen injury to roses planted near edges of rose beds mainly during open, cold winters where there has not been an adequate snow cover. Under severe winter conditions, even the roses in the center of the bed can be injured. However, the injury is usually no more severe than roses growing directly in the ground.

When properly constructed and maintained, raised beds can turn an otherwise poor gardening area into an attractive bed of roses.

Starting Seeds Indoors

Fred Glasoe

Fluorescent lights have made it possible for gardeners to fill their planter-boxes with colorful annuals they have grown indoors from seed. Anyone can get a good garden started under a two or four-tube fluorescent light fixture. All you need is the fixture, chains to adjust the height of the tubes, an on-off timer, some trays, and a sterile soil blend.

March is the high point for indoor seeding of annuals. Although some of our flowers were started in January and February, the bulk of our outdoor bloom should get its start during March. This allows the plants to get big enough to give you a head start in the garden without outgrowing their pots before transplanting.

Here are the basics of successfully growing your own annuals from seed:

1. Seeding trays must be clean. Wash them in hot, soapy water and soak them at least ten minutes in a solution of one part bleach to nine parts water.

2. Make sure to use a sterile soil mix. Your local garden center carries brands such as Jiffy Mix or Pro Mix. Never use old soil. Any yeast, mold, or other fungal spores which might have made their way into the soil will cause "damping off", a common disease which kills the sprouted seed.

3. The moisture level of the seeding mix is very important. One common mistake is sowing seeds in a dry medium and then watering. This produces the likelihood that the seed will be washed away, covered up with eroding soil, or floated down the drain if you place the dry seed tray into a pan of water. Seed-starting media must never dry out and yet must not remain too wet. Fill your seed trays or pots with your sterile seed-starting mix, water them thoroughly, and allow them to stand out of the water and drain overnight. This produces a dampness that is just right for seeding.

4. You are now ready to seed. Fine seeds can be dusted evenly over the top, but larger seeds can be spaced along the bottom of small "furrows" formed by

pressing a ruler or similar object into the soil. Sow lightly, using only a few seeds per seed box. Use several small containers rather than one big one to help prevent a wipe-out from damping off. Cover the container(s) with a piece of glass or slip the trays into a clear plastic bag and seal with a twist-tie. This step is necessary to retain moisture.

5. A good indoor seeding climate includes both good light and warm temperatures to promote germination. After the seed has germinated, the plastic wrap or glass should be opened at one end and gradually removed completely over the next week to ten days.

6. Do not let your newly germinated seedlings get too large before you transplant them. Two sets of "true" leaves is just the right size for transplanting. I plant six or eight plants in a seeding tray, keep a plastic bag over the tray and keep it out of strong light for three to five days. This helps insure strong root development. Once young plants are transplanted, they grow best in a cool climate with good light intensity. A set of fluorescent lights in your cool basement is ideal for early seedlings. Most seedlings like an 18-hour light period with 6 hours of darkness. Keep the lights at five to eight inches above the seedlings. Never move the light source more than 12 inches from the seedlings.

7. Fertilize your seedlings with a mild solution of a water-soluble fertilizer such as Miracle-Gro. Use a one-quarter strength solution every other watering. Try to be gentle when watering.

8. Window sills and sunny porches often receive enough April sun so that they can be used as growing areas for seedlings. A good environment has full-day sun and cool temperatures. If this is not the situation on your porch or windowsills, continue using fluorescent lights in the cool basement until plants can be put outside on warm days and brought into an indoor garage or porch on below-freezing nights. Watch out for leaf sunburn: artificial light does not condition a plant to natural sunlight. Seedlings must be eased into early morning or late afternoon sun and kept out of the intense mid-day sun for the first week after they are set outdoors.

By mid-May you will have many plants to set out, you will have saved money, and you will have a much wider selection than that offered by your local garden center.

Growing Alpines in Containers

Alpines" is a general name used for the smallest rock plants, almost all under six inches in height. Because these plants are small and are difficult to see in a regular perennial garden bed, you will best be able to enjoy their beauty by planting them together in a special setting of some kind.

Hypertufa troughs and planters are natural homes for these small wonders and make a unique accent piece for your garden. Hypertufa is a mix of cement, peatmoss, and vermiculite that can be formed to make a wide variety of stone-like garden planters. The finished piece is lighter in weight than real stone, weathers nicely, and provides these miniature perennials with the special growing conditions they need to flourish. These containers are a great feature for a patio or terrace.

One advantage of our colder climate and snowy winters is that it approximates the natural growing climate of the mountain alpine plants. True alpine plants are natives of mountain heights above the tree line and the higher you go, the shorter the summer and the

growing season of the plants. Alpines have compensated for these extremes in climate by being able to grow at low temperatures and by growing very early in the spring.

On the following pages are instructions for building a small hypertufa planter and some suggestions on easy-to-grow alpines.

This hypertufa planter provides a natural alpine showcase. (Shannon)

Gardening Skill

How to build a small hypertufa planter.

To make a small hypertufa planter you need something to use as a basic form or mold. For irregular shapes, you can use a firm pile of damp fine-grained sand. Or you can use old dishpans, large bowls, or any other item that has the size and shape you want for your garden.

Ingredients and Proportions

An easy to use and lighter-weight mixture is comprised of the following materials:

> 1 part pure Portland cement (do not use a pre-mix cement which contains gravel)

> 1 1/2 parts peat moss (sift to remove larger chunks)

> 1 1/2 parts Vermiculite (try Perlite or course sand for different textures)

> 1 part shredded fiber mesh (available at lumber centers)

Cement coloring powders come in shades of brown, black, yellow, and green. Start with 1/2 cup per quart of cement and adjust to your preference. Experiment!

Tools & Equipment

- rubber gloves
- container to measure ingredients
- pan to mix the hypertufa ingredients together
- plastic garbage bags (to line the mold)
- short dowels
- wire brush
- chisel
- fiber mesh
- cement coloring powders (if desired)

Getting Started

The hypertufa mixture can be applied to the inside or outside of many molds. Take into consideration that if applied to the outside, your finished planter will have the same interior space as your mold. If applied to the inside, your planter will have a smaller interior space. Here are instructions for a small trough planter:

1. Start by picking a suitable mold and lining the surface with plastic to keep the mix from sticking to the mold.

2. Mix the sifted peat moss and Vermiculite together. Add the Portland cement and mix well. Now you can add colorant if desired.

3. Add water slowly. Stir until the mixture binds together. You can add more water a little at a time if the mixture becomes too firm as you work.

4. Pack the bottom of the mold with about 1 1/2 inches of your mix. Make some drainage holes in the bottom by pushing in short 1/2 inch diameter dowels. Start building up the side walls. These should be about 2 inches thick.

5. Allow the cement to harden for 12 to 48 hours. It should be firm but scratchable with a fingernail. Pull out the dowels with a twisting motion and remove the planter from the mold.

6. To "age" your hypertufa container and give it the feel of real stone, nick it with a chisel and give it a good scouring with a wire brush. Brush off any remaining crumbs with a soft brush.

7. Allow the cement to continue "curing" by covering it for a week or two with a sheet of plastic. Then allow the planter to "weather" and the lime in the cement to neutralize by placing it outside for four to six weeks. Avoid direct sunlight or temperatures below freezing.

8. Finally, burn off any fiberglass stubs with a propane torch.

Seeds for Thought

Easy-to-grow alpines for trough gardens.

Allysum

Androsace primuloides

Arabis – Also known as rock cress. Produces a sheet of white or pink flowers in May.

Crocus, wild species

Dwarf Dianthus – Dianthus are charming, easy plants for beginners. Their colors and forms are highly variable. Many varieties.

Draba – A gem of an alpine that is long-lived and dependable. Yellow flowers bloom in earliest spring.

Hardy Geraniums – Many shades of pink, purple, and red.

Helianthemum

Hepatica – Blue-white flowers with beautiful three-lobed leaves.

Papaver alpinum

Creeping phlox – Cushions of flowers in spring; many colors. Some varieties will take light shade.

Sedum – Easy to grow, long-lived succulents; many interesting types available.

Sempervivum – Commonly called "Hens and Chicks." They originated on mountains where their outer leaves protect the inner heart from drought and cold.

Creeping Thyme – Thymes are invaluable creeping plants thickly clothed with minute leaves. In June they are covered with flowers in shades of pink, rose, and white.

Saxifages – Saxifages look like delicate "Hens and Chicks." They are in the premier alpine plant for a slightly shaded location in our climate.

Dwarf Veronicas – Many varieties with flower colors of blue, pink, and white.

If your local garden center does not carry the alpines you want, you can order from:

Rice Creek Gardens
11506 Highway 65
Blaine, MN 55434

For additional information on alpines and rock gardening, you may wish to join the American Rock Garden Society. For details, write to:

Secretary
ARGS
P.O. Box 67
Millwood, NY 10546

THE NORTHERN GARDENER'S LIBRARY

Chapter 3

Plants for Containers

Potted Perennials

Growing Fruits in Containers

Alpine Strawberries

Hanging Baskets

Vegetable Varieties for Containers

Suggestions for Raised Beds

A Balcony Planting List

Plants to Attract Wildlife

Potted Perennials

Robert Estelle

ardy perennials, grown as specimens in containers, can be both productive and beautiful. They can also be extremely challenging, testing horticultural knowledge and skill. There's little to lose by trying, however, and success brings both satisfaction and a beautiful addition to the landscape.

A small conifer, a flowering shrub, or a fruiting bush, can—with care—be grown permanently in a container of moderate size. It's an excellent way to learn about fertilization, watering, pruning, and about protection from summer sun and winter cold. A knowledge of propagation, too, may be useful for those who wish to acquire or to multiply perennials for growing in containers.

Wintering

Perennials that can be wintered in the open ground by burying the root ball and mulching with straw are the most satisfactory subjects for beginning experiments. Even hardy container-grown perennials, however, are vulnerable during northern winters. The root system must not be allowed to dry out

completely and must be protected from repeated freezing and thawing, which means that the container must not be left above ground, unprotected and exposed to sun and wind.

The simplest and surest method of wintering potted perennials is burying the root ball, in most cases without the container. If the container is ornamental and costly, one will surely want to remove it, without damaging the ball of soil and roots. Even a plastic nursery container will prevent the earth ball from absorbing moisture from the surrounding soil and could cause desiccation of the plant. Also the rim of the container forms a dam, trapping water that will freeze around the base of the plant and could be damaging.

Gardeners who prefer not to remove the containers should set the container into the soil so deeply that the rim is at least two inches below ground level. Cover the base of the plant and the rim of the pot with an ample mound of earth, rising several inches above the general level of the surrounding soil. This will keep ice from forming at the base of the plant, while helping to retain moisture. A mulch of hay or straw (but no plastic or other waterproof covering) should be added above the mound of soil for extra protection. The area where plants are set into the ground for wintering should be well drained and protected from wind and direct sunlight.

Types of Plants

Not all perennials are equally suitable for continuing growth in containers. It is probably best to avoid plants which grow very rapidly or become very large. Begin with plants whose normal form is that of a low bush or small tree.

This would include dwarf evergreens, low berry bushes, ornamental shrubs, or trees which are ordinarily small. It is not necessary to invest in trees grown on dwarf rootstocks, because we hope to control the growth by other means. Suitable plants, other than small conifers, might be gooseberry or currant bushes, lowbush blueberries, a dwarf 'North Star' cherry tree, a western bush cherry, floribunda roses, a 'Miss Kim' lilac, hardy azaleas, or French hybrid grapes.

Pruning

Pruning, both of roots and top growth, is the principal means

A patio of this size would be the perfect place to try growing flowering shrubs or fruiting bushes in containers. (Emerson)

used to control the size and shape of container plantings. Through pruning of top growth one can shape the plant, training it in an oriental pattern, in some form of European espalier or in some more modern free style. After the first year's growth, decide on an ultimate size, both for the container and for the plant. When the tree or shrub moves into a 10 or 12-inch container to begin its second or third year of growth, it can be maintained at that size indefinitely. This will require an annual pruning of the root system after the ground has thawed, but before active spring growth begins. Top pruning should be continued, both to maintain a balance between root and top growth, as well to maintain the desired shape.

Special tubs with removable sides have been designed to facilitate root pruning. With such containers, the plant does not have to be lifted out of the tub, as would be the case if it were grown in an ordinary nursery container. If the plant is very big, growing in a large amount of soil, a container with removable sides will make pruning of the roots much easier. If the nursery container is no larger than 12 inches in diameter, the root ball can usually be removed intact, without damage and without great difficulty.

The root-pruning process consists of cutting away a slice of earth from one or, at most, two sides of the soil mass. The soil should not be too wet or too dry, so that it will neither ooze nor crumble. Each slice should be made vertically, completely through the soil from top to bottom, and its greatest thickness should be less than two inches for plants growing in 12-inch, round containers. For square containers of comparable size, no slice should be more than one inch thick at any point. Cut away only one slice if root growth has been moderate and has not filled the soil around the outside of the earth mass.

After root pruning, the plant should be returned to the container and new soil tamped firmly into place at the edges. New roots will grow in this added soil during the coming summer. Next spring take slices of earth from the sides that were not pruned this year. Scraping away and replacing any loose soil from the top of the earth ball will be beneficial, if one is careful not to damage roots lying near the surface. Enough new soil should be added so that the container is filled to within an inch of its rim in order to protect and fertilize the roots.

Growing Fruits in Containers

Robert Estelle

he northern states are not the nation's fruit basket, but that is no reason not to experiment with grapes or gooseberries in your back yard. For varieties that are hardy and compact, container gardening is an ideal solution that offers the protection and flexibility that our northern winters sometimes deny. Among the best choices are blueberries, gooseberries, Alpine strawberries, and perhaps best of all, grapes. All are decorative, as well as tasty.

Blueberries

'Northblue' and 'Northsky', developed at the University of Minnesota, are reliably hardy blueberries that rival wild berries for taste, but have a much lower growth habit, so snow can protect the flower buds. Both are ideal for home landscaping, with glossy foliage that turns dark red in the fall. They are great possibilities for growing in containers as decorative food plants.

Gooseberries

Gooseberries are also a good choice for container gardeners who are looking for unusual fruit varieties. Even in its wild form, it is an interesting and rewarding subject for experiment. In improved forms, it has been grown for many years in Europe and now in the United States. Familiar garden varieties include 'Pixwell' and 'Welcome', which are hardy, reliable plants for northern gardeners.

Other types with larger, more attractive, and tastier fruit have been grown in England and in northern Europe, though they have not always grown satisfactorily in the northern United States. Five varieties seem particularly worthy of experimental growth in containers: 'Captivator', a completely thornless Canadian berry, light-red to full-red fruit, delicious flavor; 'Canada 0-273', relatively thornless, medium to large, copper-red fruit, high quality; 'Hinnomaki Yellow' and 'Lepaa Red', two superb Finnish varieties—Hinnomaki has very large, smooth, shiny yellowish-green berries with a rich, sweet taste, while Lepaa has large, red berries of high quality; and 'Poorman', relatively small, pear-shaped berries, dark wine red, one of the most delicious.

With such descriptions, who could resist the temptation to try one or more of these unusual varieties of gooseberry?

Alpine Strawberry

The Alpine strawberry, with sweet fruit of small to medium size, resembles the North American wild strawberry, but is of European origin. It is quite ornamental and often grown in flower borders. It does not spread intrusively beyond its bounds, and its blossoms and fruit are held fairly high, within or above the foliage, where they can be admired by the gardener and where they are safe from soil-borne pests and diseases. Oddly enough, the visibility of the fruit does not seem to make them especially vulnerable to damage by birds, perhaps because they are not native. Another advantage offered by these strawberries is their ever-bearing habit. They fruit continuously from June until frost.

Alpine strawberries are most economically, and rather easily, grown from seed. If started early enough indoors they will fruit in August of the same season, but they will give a full summer of fruit the following year and for years thereafter. They are hardy, though if they are grown in containers, it is best to group them together in a secure cold frame for the winter.

Seeds of several varieties are available, as are plants. Varieties include 'Delices', an improved 'Monstreuse Caennaise'; 'Baron Solemacher'; and 'Pineapple Crush', with creamy, yellow berries.

Grapes

The grapevine is one of the most decorative plants that a home gardener can grow—the attractions are various. Some will be fascinated by the historical importance of the grape, which reaches back into ancient times. Others will be attracted by the vine's inherent beauty, by the ease with which it can be trained into decorative forms, or by the great number of species and available varieties. Not the least of the grapevine's attractive features are its low cost and its ease of propagation.

The grapevine is not normally grown in containers. Many midwestern gardeners think of grape vines as an enormous mass of woody trunks, covering a decaying shed or fence, controllable only by pruning away large portions with an ax. It is seldom thought of as a dainty, well-trained, ornamental plant, regularly bearing fruit. The grapevines with which we are familiar are reliably hardy, can survive total neglect, and are enormous, sprawling, vigorous plants. Their occasional fruit is not very tasty when eaten fresh, makes poor wine, and is chiefly used for giving a blue color to grape jelly. Vines which require training and some winter protection are available, however, and these can, with a little effort on our part, open up a whole new world of viticultural experience.

The most interesting varieties to choose for container growing are French-American hybrids, such as 'Aurora', 'Baco Noir', 'Cascade', 'De Chaunac', or 'Foch'. These hybrids have the mystique and wine-producing qualities of the French varieties, along with the disease resistance of the American types. Most American varieties are usually considered table grapes, rather than wine grapes, and include 'Caco', 'Concord', 'Edelweiss', 'Fredonia', 'Interlaken Seedless', 'Niagara', and 'Swenson's Red'.

In container culture, the vine's trunk, or the permanent part of the vine, should be kept quite short, perhaps just a few inches above the root. Each year, grow a sufficient number of good canes from a point close to the upper end of the trunk. Next year, these are the canes that will produce fruit. In the fall, after the grapes are harvested, these canes, still carrying the now useless shoots which bore the grapes, will be cut off next to the trunk. The new canes which were encouraged to grow this year from the top of the trunk, will be preserved and bear next summer's

'Swenson's Red' is considered a table grape. (MSHS)

crop. In other words, grapes are produced on shoots which sprout from the buds on last year's growth. This growth is then discarded (or used as cuttings for new vines), while new growth provides the buds for next year's fruit-producing shoots.

Keeping the trunk short will facilitate winter protection. Whenever possible, shoots from the upper part of the trunk should be pruned at a point just above the second or third bud beyond their base, in order to make each single branch into a double one. If the grapevine is a new, unbranched cutting, cut it back during dormancy to two or three buds in order to induce branching.

When vines are planted in the open ground and attached to a trellis, it is usual to have fewer, but longer, fruiting canes, but a container-grown vine may be easier to handle and more decorative with a larger number of short canes. They should not be too short, however. For most American and French hybrid grapes, the fruiting canes must be five buds or more in length, because the first two or three buds, closest to the base of the cane, will not give rise to fruit-bearing shoots. Remember that the greater the number of fruiting canes, the more replacement spurs one should provide.

The canes that hold this summer's fruit can be tied on a fan-shaped trellis, leaving room at the center of the trellis for the new canes growing from the renewal spurs. These new canes will grow most vigorously if they are tied vertically, in the center of the trellis. Each of the fruit-bearing shoots, sprouting from the buds on last year's canes, can be pinched off after they have formed a flower cluster or two, to keep within the room allowed by the trellis and to encourage strong growth from the renewal spurs, insuring productive canes for next year's fruit.

Winter protection is best given by removing the dormant vine from its trellis in October or November, pruning away the canes which fruited during the past summer, and carefully bundling together the canes that will bear next year's fruit. The pot can be set into a hole in the garden, and leaves, straw, or other insulating material packed around all parts of the vine. In many cases, merely setting the potted vine into a deep cold frame, with some straw around the pot, will afford sufficient protection.

A 12-inch nursery container should be large enough to grow most grapevines. The French-American hybrids seem a little less rampant than some of the purely American vines. Growing a grapevine in a container permits those of us who are renters, apartment dwellers, or unsettled nomads to enjoy the aesthetic and scientific delights of viticulture.

In addition to added aesthetic benefits, all of the fruits mentioned are great for eating and cooking. Outdoor containers of blueberries and gooseberries will help attract wildlife, drawing many species of birds for your viewing enjoyment. Container gardening provides a sheltered, controlled environment that allows gardeners great freedom in choosing which fruits to try in their home landscape.

Alpine Strawberries

Robert Estelle

he Alpine strawberry is one of the most delightful of all plants to grow in containers. It is small and pretty, fitting neatly into a six-inch pot. The bright green leaves, the white flowers, and the red fruit are held above the soil on thin, strong stems. The plant has a much more delicate appearance and is more erect than the commonly grown garden strawberry which has runners and tends to sprawl. The Alpine strawberry has no runners and its fruits are held well above the plant, as if on display. Because it has such an appearance of tall, slender aristocracy, it is hard to believe that the Alpine strawberry is extremely hardy, easy to grow, and — above all — delicious.

The Alpine strawberry varieties are cultivated forms of the wild European strawberry *Fragaria vesca* with the added denomination of *semperflorens* or *sempervirens*. The usual garden or commercial strawberries are hybrids, combining forms of the North American *Fragaria virginiana* and the South American *F. chiloensis*. The fruit of the Alpine strawberry is not as large as that of the hybrid commer-cial kinds familiar to most garden-ers, but it is appreciably larger than the native wild strawberry, still to be found in Minnesota in wooded areas. The Alpine strawberry is con-sidered to be extremely tasty and has acquired something of a repu-tation as a select fruit for gourmets.

Alpine strawberries are rather easily grown from seed and are inexpensive when raised in that way. In March or April, the seed should be sown by sprinkling them on top of moist vermiculite. The seeding containers should be placed where they can receive light during the day, at a temperature of 55° to 70°F until the seeds germi-nate. The seeds are small and should not be covered. They sprout irregularly, taking from two to four weeks. One should be careful not to disturb the seeds by careless water-ing. As soon as the plants are large enough to handle, transplant them from vermiculite into soil in two-inch pots where they can remain until transferring them to six-inch pots in May or June. The young plants must not be allowed to freeze, of course, but they will grow well in cool temperatures. The soil

61

should be well drained and there should be good air movement around the plants, but the soil must not be allowed to dry out completely between waterings.

Because the Alpine strawberry is a woodland plant, it can be grown successfully all summer in partial (but not deep) shade. If seeded in March, the plants should start producing berries in August, continuing until frost or, if protected, until November. The following year, if given some protection during the winter, they will begin bearing in June.

It is evidently not necessary to protect the plants from birds, who are often attracted to the ripening berries of the usual garden strawberries. Despite (or, perhaps, because of) the fact that the fruit are held on erect stems, above the leaves, they are not bothered. This is mentioned in British books which describe Alpine strawberries, and it seems to be borne out by experience here in Minnesota.

In late August or early September, each year, the crowns can be divided into two or three times that number of plants, each plant having developed a second or a third crown. The plants, because they do not send out runners, must be propagated vegetatively by division of the crowns. The danger in repeated vegetative propagation of Alpine strawberries lies in their possible susceptibility to virus infections from aphids. Alpine strawberries have not been bred for disease resistance and they may develop infections over a period of several years. Propagating new plants from seed every few years will avoid a continued succession of declining plants.

Alpine strawberries are quite hardy and normally need no special protection, but if they are in pots, the pots should be set into the ground before it freezes or they should be grouped in a coldframe and protected with straw. The plants *do* need a dormant period and will not grow indefinitely if brought into the house in August or September. It is best to winter them outside and to bring them into the house in the spring, rather than in the fall, if you want a fruit-bearing conversation piece in April or May. This is a tricky business, but if you have some experience in forcing bulbs, for instance, forcing strawberries should seem easy enough. Naturally, there is no problem in bringing potted strawberries indoors any time during the summer if proper growing conditions are provided while they are in the house.

Alpine strawberries are not yet well known in the United States, but are a favorite delicacy in England and on the European continent, especially in France where they are known as *fraises des bois* or "woodland strawberries." They are usually eaten fresh, with sugar and cream. They supposedly have a higher pectin content than the American commercial strawberry and, therefore, are especially suited to making jam. However, they are too delicious and seldom so plentiful that one would ever really consider cooking them up as jam. They are a bright, glossy red when ripe and have an interesting elongated, bumpy shape. There is a variety with yellow berries and it might be almost excessively elegant to serve the yellow and the red fruits mixed, as a dessert for guests.

An ideal container plant should be small and easily manageable; should have decorative foliage, attractive flowers, and eye-catching fruit; should continue to blossom and fruit for months at a time; should be inexpensive to acquire; should be easy to propagate and grow; should be unusual and not too common; should be hardy; should bear in the same season as it is seeded; and should adapt well to container culture. The Alpine strawberry fits all these requirements. It is an ideal plant for the container gardener.

Seeds For Thought

Container Types

Clay. Clay pots include both terra-cotta and earthenware. Unglazed pots can become crusted with salt or coated with algae which can be kept under control with a regular cleaning program. Clay pots are susceptible to cracking, so more care is required. Unglazed pots are porous, which helps keep the roots cool and allows for the exchange of air and moisture. Clay pots are a natural-looking addition to the garden.

Cement. A wider assortment of cast cement and sculpted stone containers are now available. They are very durable but are also much heavier than clay.

Plastic. If you are concerned about weight, use plastic. Plastic pots now come in a variety of new designs as well as the traditional tapered-with-rim look. Compared to clay pots, plastic pots lose less water, but don't get as much air. Therefore, you may want to experiment with a lighter soil mix if using plastic.

Ceramic. Decorative ceramic pots are the most expensive choice but offer the widest design possibilities. Glazed pots come in many colors and shapes. They are very durable. If the ceramic pot you like does not have drainage holes, you may want to consider double-potting.

Hanging Baskets

Robert Estelle

Many ornamental annuals are grown regularly in hanging baskets, but this is not as commonly done with fruits and vegetables, with the possible exception of the tomato, some varieties of which are advertised as being suitable for culture in hanging baskets. Cucumbers, small melons, and gourds can be raised in suspended containers. Because these tend to grow as true vines, they may be trained in festoons, looping the vine back up to the edge of the container and passing it inside one of the supporting cords, allowing the end to grow downward again. If the fruit are very heavy, they may require support on shelves or in slings. Pole beans and peas, despite their vining habit, may not be leafy enough to make an attractive display, although they can be trained up the cords that support the container, rather than allowed to hang beneath.

New Zealand spinach, a trailing, hot-weather spinach substitute, is certainly adaptable to growth in hanging baskets. A number of plants are not really recumbent, but their older, outer stems and leaves tend to lie flat against the earth. If grown in pots, their leaves can be allowed to reach beyond the perimeter of the container, where they can hang down but remain dry. Some vegetables which we would not ordinarily consider growing in hanging containers may, indeed, benefit from being raised this way. These would include lettuces, cabbage, spinach, carrots, beets, and some types of bushy peppers.

Certain popular herbs, such as parsley, chives, mint, and borage, are ideal for hanging baskets. Chives and parsley, despite their generally upright habit, tend to produce tall stems which fall and form a larger clump as the plants grow. Many herbs should be grown, at least experimentally, in hanging containers, to keep their lovely scents more nearly at nose level.

Fruits for hanging baskets include perennial vines or sprawling bushes, such as gooseberries or currants and, certainly, grapes. The sprawling habit of gooseberries and currants would no longer be a problem but an asset, if these

Many annuals such as these impatiens are regularly grown in hanging baskets. The author suggests vegetables and herbs that also might be appropriate. (Rogers)

plants were grown in suspended pots.

The strawberry is the fruit most commonly grown in unorthodox containers. It can very well be grown in hanging pots, with runners falling decoratively over the edge. Also it is often grown in the pockets of tall clay containers, called strawberry jars.

Hanging baskets offer plants better access to air and light. Baskets can be hung from a hook fastened to any overhead support. The lower limbs of trees may seem to provide a logical place to hang containers, but trees often harbor a great many insects, all of which will inevitably fall onto the plants. Insufficient sunlight and excessive debris, such as twigs and leaves, are additional drawbacks. If your yard lacks ideal places to hang baskets, consider constructing simple tripods to hold plants aloft.

Seeds For Thought

Larger hanging baskets can get very heavy, especially after watering. Always make sure your hangers will support the full weight of the basket, the plants, and water.

Vegetable Varieties for Containers

Robert Estelle

he following varieties have been grown satisfactorily in containers in zone four gardens. Most of these selections have been grown successfully for ten or more years. There are always new introductions suitable for container gardening, but here is a list of some tried and true varieties.

Beans Try green or wax pole beans with a trellis attached to the

Pole beans are great for a small-space vegetable garden. (AAS)

container. Good pole bean varieties are 'Romano Italian' (green) and 'Burpee Golden' (yellow). Bush beans are not quite as prolific or showy, but still very worthwhile. There are lots of good varieties. I have grown 'Burpee's Tenderpod' (green) and 'Goldcrop' (yellow).

Beets and Carrots Not very ornamental crops, but worthwhile if you can arrange for a well-drained, loose soil mix. Try early-maturing varieties with short roots and pick them young. Use beet tops as greens. For carrots, 'Spartan Bonus', 'Goldinhart', and 'Sweetheart' have done well, and for beets, 'Ruby Queen', but there are many other varieties to try.

Cabbage I am surprised by the number of people who have confessed to me that they have never seen a cabbage actually growing in the ground. Why not grow a head or two to show the kids (and the neighbors) what they look like outside the supermarket? 'Early Golden Acre' and 'Green Acre' develop well in containers. They have to be started from seed around March 15 in order to be ready to plant out in late May. Cabbages are not very ornamental nor productive for containers, but they are interesting and instructive.

Cucumbers The vine crops, such as cucumbers, squash, and melons, have been the object of much breeding and selection in order to make them more compact. These efforts to reduce the distance between the plants' nodes have been aimed largely at fitting the plants to smaller gardens. However, many people feel that the form of such plants also makes them more suitable for growth in containers. I recommend trying both bush types and vining varieties with a trellis.

'Bush Champion', 'Spacemaster', 'Park's Burpless Bush', 'Bush Whopper', and 'Patio Pik' are all options for bush types in containers. 'Burpee's Burpless' is an absolute must on a trellis, so that the cucumbers grow long and straight. It has very decorative vines, delicious fruit for slicing, and is one of the best container vegetables. It should be started indoors about the middle of April for early June transplanting.

Eggplant Although not a staple in many gardens, it is very attractive and can be grown in containers. There are small-fruited types, which grow on sturdy, bushy plants. Of these, the variety 'Morden Midget' is highly rated. Start plants indoors at the beginning of April for transplanting to outdoor containers early in June.

Herbs Plant a large box with chives, dill, marjoram, parsley, sage, summer savory, thyme, and others. They contrast nicely when grown together, and are fun to pick, pinch, smell, taste, and admire.

Lettuce This is my favorite container crop. The types (Bibb, Leaf, Romaine, Crisphead) and varieties within each type give enormous opportunities for experiment at low cost. Plant in low wooden containers, which are four to six inches deep and a foot or two in length and width. There is no

Cucumbers come in both bush and vining types. Try both! (AAS)

You can enjoy a salad of fresh lettuce greens year-round. (MSHS)

better way to make a salad of tender, fresh, tasty greens than by picking those you have grown yourself. Even buying them at a farmer's market is not as satisfactory. 'Black Seeded Simpson' seems to me to be the most successful leaf lettuce, but try also 'Oak Leaf', 'Ruby', and 'Salad Bowl'. 'Paris White' and 'Sweet Midget' are good Romaine, or Cos, lettuces. 'Buttercrunch Bibb' grows well. Crisphead lettuce presents some difficulty in growing, but the standard variety 'Great Lakes' is a good one to start. I grow lettuce every month of the year, in containers indoors or out, and enjoy it immensely, both as a decorative

and culinary treat. It is my one indispensable container plant!

Melons One of the most interesting and enjoyable container crops, but not the easiest or most productive. Melons should be started indoors about the middle of April and put outside the first week in June. A trellis is needed, and the fruit will have to be supported on shelves or by slings. A container of at least five gallon capacity is needed and regular watering is required. There are so many small melons, some of which have been developed for early ripening and confined spaces. Also, some oriental melons, which do not "slip" (loosen from the stem when ripe) and can be grown like cucumbers, are available. I have not grown these, but I understand that they are not as highly flavored as the cantaloupe melons. Melons that have been grown fairly successfully in containers include 'Chaca Number One', 'Hybrid Charentais', 'Minnesota Midget', 'Ha Ogen', 'Minnesota Honeymist', 'New Hampshire Midget', and 'Yellow Baby'. The last two are small watermelons. All of these melons grow on vines, but despite the necessity for a trellis, vine vegetables seem easier to manage in containers than do bush types. However, as with cucumbers, container gardeners should try both and see which they prefer. Among compact, short-internode melons are

'Oliver's Pearl Cluster Honeydew', 'Busheloupe', and 'Short 'N' Sweet', all designed for gardens with limited space, and the third specifically recommended for container culture. Growing melons off the ground avoids many of the problems usually encountered in traditional gardening. Perhaps because they are one of my favorite things to eat, melons remain one of my favorite things to grow.

Okra Usually not considered an ideal container plant, because it is ordinarily too tall and too sparse to be decorative. However its very pretty hibiscus-like flowers and the interesting shape of its fruit make it an intriguing plant. 'Lee' is an early okra of compact form. Its fruits are spineless, and the branches and fruit are rather close together along the stalk. A suitable choice for container growing by those who demand that their vegetables be both decorative and edible.

Onions Very easy to grow and most worthwhile if grown as green onions for salad use or summer cooking. It makes less sense to try to grow them to maturity as dry onions. Use onion sets to save trouble, although seeding works fine, either directly outside in May or earlier for transplanting. Pull the onions and use, tops and all, when young and nicely green.

Peppers In many ways, peppers are the ideal vegetable for container gardeners who insist that their plants be decorative as well as fruitful. Along with tomatoes, they share the honor of being the most adapted to container growing, the most decorative, the most diverse in their varieties, and the most useful for cooking. Most peppers are self-supporting and do not require poles or trellises. They should be started indoors in early April for transplanting to unprotected areas in the first week of June. Choose both hot and sweet peppers, and select some for their shape and color. My favorites include 'California Wonder' (sweet, green); 'Sweet Banana' (sweet, yellow); 'Large Cherry' (hot, green to red, round shape); and 'Hungarian Wax' (hot, yellow to red). The variety 'Dutch Treat' is a small-fruited sweet pepper, turning from yellow to orange to red, with fruit held above the foliage—very pretty! In addition, there are a great number of smaller plants, sold as ornamental peppers, which are delightful and capable of being dried and ground as a seasoning.

Radishes Advocated as an ideal vegetable for container gardening, they are by no means foolproof. Sow them sparsely so that the remaining radishes will not be disturbed by thinning. Protect the container from the direct heat of the sun and make sure it's deep enough to accommodate the root. Grow round rather than long radishes, use a loose soil mix with good drainage, and keep them well watered. The main appeal of radish growing is the short time to maturity. 'Cherry Belle' is a good variety, but there are many others.

Spinach and other greens Mustard and spinach substitutes (New Zealand Spinach, Malabar Spinach, and Tampala) are perhaps the most interesting and useful. Growing ordinary spinach is difficult, and container gardening does not reduce the difficulties. Swiss chard, in both its red-stemmed form ('Burpee's Rhubarb') and its white-stemmed form ('Fordhook'), is very decorative. Chards are very nutritious, as are all greens.

Strawberries Although you may not classify these as vegetables, they are an ideal container crop. They give a fair yield, they are decorative, they are hardy, and they are fairly easy to grow and even to multiply by asexual propagation. You can grow any of the standard June-bearing or ever-bearing varieties, but I propose that you try the smaller, tastier, and very prolific Alpine strawberries, which can be grown from seed. These do not produce runners, but the crowns can be divided every year or two. They are perennial and will survive northern winters with minimal protection. The variety 'Baron Solemacher' is commonly sold as seed. Start the seed indoors in early March and plants should have berries the first summer. They fruit, thereafter, from early spring to late fall. I've had berries as late as November from potted plants kept in a cold frame. Alpine strawberries are often used, like ornamental pepper plants, for their decorative effect in flower gardens.

Squash Summer squashes, especially zucchini, are my choice for growing in containers. Zucchini varieties tend to be more compact than other types, but there are also compact forms of butternut and acorn squash, as well as zucchini. 'Butterbush' and 'Early Acorn Hybrid' are good winter types, as is 'Jersey Golden Acorn'. The larger winter squashes require lots of room for roots and lots of water, and their vines and fruit are generally too heavy for easy trellising. The prolific zucchini is small in size. Try 'Park's Creamy', a yellow zucchini. 'Aristocrat' and 'Fordhook' are two good green varieties. Zucchini, like cucumbers, are valuable container plants and will repay all your effort and care.

Tomatoes Of the stiff, upright tomatoes developed for growing in pots, one of the best known is 'Pixie Hybrid'. It has been offered for some years as an ideal tomato for small gardens, flower borders, or containers. It is an early, attractive, and reliable plant which holds itself upright with little or no artificial support. 'City Best' is a tomato of similar growth form, a determi-

There are many varieties of tomatoes suitable for decks or balconies. (AAS)

its intended use. 'Goldie', an indeterminate plant yielding clusters of small, attractive yellow fruit, is ideal for growing in a hanging basket, as is 'Minibel', a red companion. 'Toyboy' is a small, red-fruited tomato, for hanging basket culture.

Other tomatoes usually considered to be container varieties include 'Tiny Tim', 'Small Fry', and 'Sugar Lump'. All have small fruit, are early, and can be grown in eight-inch pots (except for 'Small Fry', which should have two to five gallons of soil). Given a five-gallon container, almost any tomato can be grown if a suitable trellis or support is provided. Do not be afraid to experiment, and do not limit yourself to the small-fruited container types. For some gardeners, tomatoes are the only vegetable that really interests them year after year. They come in different sizes, shapes, colors, and growth habits, and all are delicious, as well as ornamental.

nate bush type, with fruit somewhat longer than the typical cherry tomato.

Vine-like tomatoes, advertised as suitable for hanging baskets, are another option, including 'Basket King Hybrid', whose name reveals

Gardening Skill

Cleaning garden pots. A good quick cleaning solution consists of one part household bleach to nine parts water. To clean crusted clay pots, use trisodium phosphate at the rate of four tablespoons per gallon of water. To make the operation easier, I will use a 15 to 20 gallon container (plastic or metal) and place the required amount of trisodium phosphate in the container and fill with water to about two-thirds capacity. *Wearing long rubber gloves*, I will carefully lower the clay pots to the bottom and allow them to soak for 12 hours. Scour with a wire rush and rinse thoroughly.   *Charlie King*

Planting Suggestions for Raised Beds

obbi and Cavour Johnson have more room in their raised beds than many of us—in the 17 different beds that make up their terraced hillside, they have about 400 square feet of actual gardening space, not counting the rock gardens on each side of the hill. For the volume-oriented gardener, even this amount of earth may not be enough. But anyone with limited space for gardens will be pleasantly surprised at the planting efficiency and yield of even one raised bed. Following is a plant list from the Johnson's, with some of their observations.

Vegetables
- Beans: both bush types and pole types were grown on the north edge of the tomato bed.
- Beets grew well in shallow beds.
- Carrots grew fairly well in shallow beds.
- Corn was grown on north edge of largest bed; it did well, but be careful to plant out of the wind, in a raised bed it won't have the protection of a larger area of corn.
- Cucumbers were trained to climb the wire fence on north edge of pepper bed; they are easier to pick if you position tiny cukes on outside of fencing.
- Kohlrabi grew well in the shallow beds.
- Onions have never done well for us, but I think we should blame our technique rather than the raised beds.
- Cherry peppers planted next to cucumbers produced a good yield.
- Green peppers didn't do as well in shallow beds but liked squash as a neighbor.
- Radishes: we harvested both early and late crops.
- Spinach was the earliest growing edible thing in our garden: two harvests.
- Squash (bush type) was planted on one side of corn bed with green peppers along another edge; it did well but would probably have liked more sun.
- Tomatoes are difficult to rotate each year in small gardens and I was fighting diseases all summer.

A Balcony Planting List

Diane Emerson

is Kelm grows both annual and perennial flowers and some tropical plants in her balcony garden. Here's a list that typifies her annual selections, as well as some of her favorite vines, shrubs, and perennial choices.

Annuals

4 flats of impatiens
15 browallias
18 tuberous begonias
36 German ivy vines
36 fibrous-rooted begonias
20 flats of petunias
18 morning glory vines
16 vinca vines
4 flats of blue salvia
10 flats of snapdragons
39 geraniums
50 to 60 zinnias
12 gerbera daisies
1 dahlia

Vines

Vines soften walls and provide height in the balcony garden. Two of Sis's favorites are 'Jackmanii', a deep purple clematis, and 'Duchess of Edinburgh', a white clematis, which she grows together. She keeps the clematis from year to year by sinking the pot into the soil in the fall.

Sis's vine collection also includes two tropicals, a six-year-old jasmine and a dipladenia. The jasmine has very fragrant white flowers and can be wintered in a garage or basement, where it goes dormant. The dipladenia (*Mandevilla splendens*), a Brazilian native, has clusters of large, pink flowers on dark green, evergreen leaves. A local greenhouse keeps Sis's vines in the winter.

Shrubs and Perennials

Sis has successfully grown roses and evergreens. The roses need to be buried in the ground over winter or covered with a lot of straw. Evergreens are tricky. To prepare them for winter, water thoroughly until hard frost, and then water again if there is a midwinter thaw.

Gardening Skill

Container Plants That Attract Wildlife

Many people do not have the option of developing a yard for wildlife. That doesn't mean they can't still attract butterflies and hummingbirds by designing a wildlife container garden for their balcony, deck, or patio. Scarlet sage (salvia) will attract ruby-throated hummingbirds throughout the spring and summer. Other container plants can help attract the over 200 butterfly species found in the Midwest.

The following list gives you plants suitable for different style containers and a wildlife value.

FLOWERS FOR HANGING BASKETS OR STRAWBERRY JARS	WILDLIFE VALUE
Waxleaf Begonia	G
Impatiens	G-EX
Petunia, Cascade Forms	EX
Nasturtium	G-EX
Garden Verbena	G
Fuchsia	G

WINDOW BOXES	
Wax Begonia	G
Impatiens	G-EX
Geranium	G
Petunia	EX
Marigold	G
Nasturtium	G-EX
Button Zinnia	EX

PLANTS FOR USE IN 4" TO 6" DIAMETER CONTAINERS	WILDLIFE VALUE
Ageratum	G
Wax Begonia	G
Sweet William	EX
China Pink	G
Hyacinth-Flowered Candytuft	G
Globe Candytuft	G
Petunia	EX
Primrose	G
Dusty Miller	G
African Marigold	G
French Marigold	G-EX
Garden Verbena	EX

Container Plants That Attract Wildlife

PLANTS FOR USE IN 8" TO 12" DIAMETER CONTAINERS	WILDLIFE VALUE
Ageratum	G
Amaryllis	EX
Heath Aster	EX
New England Aster	G
Asters	EX
Pot Marigold	EX
Canterbury Bells	EX
Annual Daisy	G
Oxeye Daisy	EX
Heliotrope	EX
Garden Balsam	G
Spotted Touch-Me-Not (jewelweed)	EX
Pale Touch-Me-Not (jewelweed)	EX
Gladiolus	EX
Daffodil	EX
Flowering Tobacco	EX
Sander Tobacco	EX
Geranium	G
Moss Pink	EX
Sweet William Phlox	G-EX
Annual Phlox	G
Summer Phlox	G
Prairie Phlox	G
Garden Sage	EX
Scarlet Sage	EX

CONTAINER GARDEN PLANTS FOR USE IN TUB OR 2-5 GALLON CONTAINERS	WILDLIFE VALUE
Rose of Sharon	EX
Geranium	G
Zinnia	G-EX
African Marigold	G-EX
French Marigold	G-EX

Wildlife Values Key:
G = Good, EX = Excellent

THE NORTHERN GARDENER'S LIBRARY

Chapter 4

Container Gardening for All Seasons

Stretching the Gardening Season

Indoor/Outdoor Hibiscus

Passion Flowers

Tropical Bulbs

Stretching the Gardening Season

Robert Estelle

Many gardeners stretch the gardening season by starting plants indoors in the spring. The other end of the summer can be stretched as well, by bringing plants inside. Don't restrict yourself to just flowering annuals or houseplants either—consider the pleasures of fresh vegetables spread out over several weeks, instead of crammed into an August glut. Vegetable gardeners are too often ignored when it comes to stretching the tail-end of the gardening season. Herbs and houseplants are often dug up and put into pots so that they can be brought indoors to continue growth in the fall. This is done less often with vegetables or fruit, but it does seem wasteful to grow a mature plant and then not to enjoy its full productive maturity. This is especially so when its productivity might well continue through the darkest and coldest months of the year.

The same fluorescent light garden or windowsill shelf used to start seeds in the spring can be home to the mature versions of those plants in the fall. The most obvious difference will be plant size, but if varieties are carefully chosen and the plants are properly supported, it will not be necessary to maintain a large indoor garden. Plan to produce only for current consumption, not for the bounty of August or for canning and freezing. A single tomato plant, for instance, would be sufficient in an indoor garden.

Plants to be brought inside for post-season growth should be prepared beforehand, beginning the previous spring. Plant them in the pots where they will grow all summer and indoors during the fall and winter. If necessary, train them on a trellis attached to the pot. The trellis and the plant should be designed to fit the indoor space they will occupy in the fall. Take special care of these plants, as they'll need to outlive those planted in traditional beds. The plant should be kept free of pests, preferably by being grown on a shelf or table, above the ground.

Whenever possible, train the plants to approximate two-dimensional, rectangular forms, with a flat surface of leaves. This will enable them to intercept a maximum amount of light at a window or in front of a series of parallel fluorescent tubes.

Choose plants that have had a full summer of growth, will continue to produce for some considerable time, and will be appreciated as a source of fresh leaves or fruit. Such plants include tomatoes, small melons, cucumbers, some herbs, alpine strawberries, passion fruit, or a citrus or fig tree. Certainly there are other plants that will prove suitable. Some, like lettuce, will be desirable, but are most easily produced by growing them from seed entirely indoors.

All plants kept beyond fall frost should be grown in containers for the entire life of the plant. They will need the advantages that special treatment and good growing conditions have given them.

The best containers are usually 10 to 12 inches in diameter and height, and be sure to use a proper soil mix. Select an indoor space and a source of light for each of the plants. It may be necessary to provide full or supplementary artificial light for some of the growing spaces.

The satisfaction that comes from being able to enjoy fresh vegetables through winter's onset cannot be overestimated. Tomatoes may be a first choice for many gardeners, but the more adventurous may prefer any number of other vegetables, or even some fruit trees suitable for growing indoors. When you select your seeds, choose some especially for late season indoor growth. It will be necessary to discover which plants will continue to produce indoors, which will grow with available light or artificial light, and which will repay us (in any sense) for our added effort. For really dedicated gardeners, questions like these are not a deterrent, but rather an incentive to experiment. If no one were willing to face difficulties, there would be no gardeners in the northern climates.

Citrus trees are a good choice to extend the growing season. (Hohman)

Indoor/Outdoor Hibiscus

Judith Hillstrom

Whether the outside temperature is 80 degrees or 18 degrees below zero, potted hibiscus offer a touch of the tropics. Bright-colored blossoms set above dark, serrated leaves contrast sharply with the northern landscape.

Container-grown hibiscus are part of a growing trend to improve the variety both for use as a house plant as well as for a garden plant.

Two favorites, both fairly recent introductions, are 'Vista' and 'Lava'. 'Vista' has three-inch frilly blooms, resembling pink silk. 'Lava', with its vibrant orange blooms, represents the advancements in continuous flowering of container-grown hibiscus. The smooth-petaled flowers have a two-day life and little or no bud drop.

Background

Hibiscus are members of the Mallow family, which includes among its 200 species okra, rose-of-sharon, cotton, and hollyhock. *Althea officinalis*, a European native and another member of the Mallow family, is the gummy root used in marshmallow-making.

In the United States, *Hibiscus coccineus* is native to Alabama, Florida, and Georgia. *H. syriacus* (althea) is grown from Florida to Ontario and west to the Rocky Mountains. These plants are perennials where temperatures remain above freezing. The more tender *Hibiscus rosa-sinensis*, the species producing the 'Vista' and 'Lava' hybrids, possesses a large gene pool

Hibiscus blossoms offer a touch of the tropics. (MSHS)

of great potential. Plant researchers are at work developing new hybrids with larger flowers, flowers with greater color range and unique shapes, and foliage of more interesting form and texture.

An ultimate goal in the breeding program is for longer-lasting blooms. Typically, flowers close umbrella-style after one or two days and drop from the plant in a few days. Later the supporting shell also falls off, making the hibiscus self-grooming.

Culture

These improved varieties bloom for four weeks, unfolding one to several blossoms each day. After this intense flowering period, the plants rest in preparation for another bloom cycle. The length of rest depends on the season of the year, the amount of light received, and day and night temperatures. Here in the far north, where winter conditions do not encourage active growth, the rest period is usually winter. But even when they are not in bloom, hibiscus make handsome indoor plants with their attractive foliage.

These made-for-container hibiscus are high-energy plants requiring very bright light when grown indoors. Give them an east, south, or west window. They also require warm temperatures for buds to develop. Bud drop or lack of development indicates insufficient light and temperatures that are too cool; move the plants to a sunnier, warmer window.

As for watering hibiscus, the soil should be kept moist, but do not allow the container to stand too long in a saucer of water. Pour water directly into the pot, letting it seep through bottom drainage holes; this leaches out soluble salts and provides the roots with oxygen. There is one drawback to a continuously moist soil: foliage on some older hibiscus varieties tends to yellow when plants are watered too frequently. Permit the hibiscus leaves to droop slightly before giving the roots a good drink. If such treatment does not solve the problem of yellow leaves, check for insects.

December through February, when plants are at natural rest and the sun travels low on the horizon, feed hibiscus only occasionally. Feed monthly using a complete and balanced fertilizer from March through November, when growing, budding, and flowering are in process.

During the summer months hibiscus are outdoor plants. This change of atmosphere is very beneficial for northern plants wintered indoors, providing them with fresh air and bright light. When moving container-grown hibiscus plants outdoors in June, it is important to ease them by stages into stronger light. Put them first on a porch so they can acclimate their tissues before moving into full sun, or else foliage burn and shock will result. Reverse these maneuvers when bringing hibiscus indoors in early September; go gradually from bright sun to less light intensity, preventing leaf and bud loss.

Grow hibiscus all summer long outdoors, potted or set in ornamental containers on a sunny patio or balcony. Plants grow, bud, and flower best in full sun with temperatures no lower than 55 degrees. Water plants the same as when grown indoors. Hibiscus may be removed from their pots and planted directly into the garden, but with the arrival of cool autumn weather they must be dug up and potted.

To repot or transplant hibiscus, use a planting mix containing two parts commercial potting soil, two parts spaghnum moss, and one part brown sand. Plant in a container eight inches or larger in diameter. Transplanting can be done at any time. Keep in mind the interior spaces where plants spend the winter—larger pots will lead to larger hibiscus.

The plants can be pruned to fit their indoor sites. Cut new plants back as soon they finish blooming, before new shoots appear. Prune older plants in early spring during the resting cycle so as not to lose a blossom on these beautiful hybrids.

Other Varieties

Selective breeding has created a number of ever-blooming hibiscus. Past introductions include 'Brilliant Red'; 'Pink Versicolor', and 'Painted Lady', both in pink shades; 'Enterpe', an apricot; 'White Red Eye'; 'Florida Sunset', an orange-bronze bicolor; 'Havana', a deep red; and 'Lemon Mist' and 'Tropic Sun', both yellows.

These new yellow hibiscus bloom in spite of high summer temperatures and are resistant to bacterial leaf spot common to yellow varieties. 'Lemon Mist' has a bright yellow flower with a red throat edged in white. 'Tropic Sun' opens dark yellow petals revealing an orange cast to its veins; its throat is pale orange and as the hours pass, the orange-peach cast turns bright yellow. In cool temperatures, the peach tone lingers to the end of the day.

Look for these varieties and others at local garden centers or florists. For more information on new introductions, write to: Yoder Brothers, Inc., P.O. Box 230, Barbarton, OH 41203.

Passion Flowers

Jim LaVigne

Although the passion flower vine *(Passiflora* spp.*)* is not hardy outdoors in zone four, it does respond well to being brought indoors for the winter. Many of my plants have survived six or seven years on this indoor-outdoor carousel. To get a passiflora to bloom is a real thrill, whether in your midsummer garden or indoors in midwinter. Passifloras are one of many tropicals or semi-tropicals prized by northern gardeners who use containers to extend both the seasons and plant varieties available to them.

My love affair with passion flowers began many years ago while visiting a greenhouse on a cold winter day. On one end of the greenhouse there was a delightful purple-flowering vine growing lush and green. The delicate-scented lavender flowers were very different from anything I'd ever seen. The gentleman who was growing these unusual vines informed me that they were *Passiflora x alato-caerulea.*

That spring I bought one plant and planted it under a trellis on the southeast corner of my garage. The vine grew rapidly and sent out many tendrils that grabbed onto the white trellis I had positioned along the garage. By early summer many showy flowers had appeared. Visitors stopped to look and ask about the purple, wheel-like flowers.

Passion flower vines thrive on an abundance of water, sun, and fertilizer. In the summer I fertilize them once a week with a 15-30-15 water-soluble fertilizer. I water them often—everyday in the heat of summer—and mist the vines to help bud formation. I provide the vines with wire or wood supports, which they quickly grow over.

After the first light frost in fall, I prune the vines back to about four feet and put them in one-gallon pots. I use a regular potting soil and am careful to include some of the soil they were growing in outdoors. I put them 6 to 12 inches away from fluorescent lights, which I leave on 12 to 14 hours a day. Fertilization with 15-30-15 begins a few weeks after they are brought indoors. The vines bud out soon thereafter, and in about December or January flowers appear. The carousel takes the vines back outdoors again in mid-May. They start out in shade and after a few days, are able to take full sun. I keep a cover handy to protect them from late spring frosts.

Passion flower vines can be propagated by cuttings taken in the fall. I have had good luck with six-inch cuttings dipped in a rooting compound and placed in potting soil inside plastic bags. Of the seven or eight passifloras I've grown over the years, my favorite is *Passiflora coccinea*.

With proper care, P. coccinea produces large, beautiful flowers. (Brown)

There are over 300 varieties of passifloras in North and South America. Others are found mainly in southeast Asia and Australia, with one being native to Madagascar. The mayprop or wild passion flower *(P. incarnata)* grows wild in the southern United States. *P. edulis* is grown extensively in Australia for its fruit, which has a pleasant taste and is about the size of a hen's egg. Many new hybrids are also being developed, and these crosses should be interesting to grow.

On a visit to northern California, I had the pleasure of seeing *Passiflora manicata* in bloom. *Passiflora manicata* has a reddish-orange blossom, about five inches across. Two or three large vines had hundreds of flowers in full bloom, and others were covered with ripe fruit. It was a photographer's field day for me, and I took dozens of photos. It is a vigorous and rapid grower, easily started from seed.

The best supplier I have found for plants is in Danielson, Connecticut. They offer 14 varieties, varying from the tiny, whitish-yellow *P. trifasciata* to the large-flowered *P. coccinea*. The plants arrive packed in spaghnum peat moss, with a foot or two of healthy vine. A copy of their catalog can be obtained by writing to the following address: Logee's Greenhouses, 55 North Street, Danielson, Connecticut 06239.

Tropical Bulbs

Emely Lincowski

As northern gardeners, we have the option of growing tropical bulbs indoors as potted plants, or outdoors in the summer as bedding or container plants. All too often these plants are overlooked simply because they are unfamiliar, even though they are fairly easy to grow. Plants such as the eye-catching clivia, a wonderfully fragrant Peruvian daffodil, or an out-of-this world blood lily make a nice change both indoors and out. Try growing them in large containers as garden accents.

Most of these plants are indigenous to tropical areas where there are distinct dry-wet weather patterns. In the north, these patterns need to be created by providing a dry resting phase when the foliage dies down—often in the fall—and the temperatures are in the 50 to 60 degree range. Some retain their foliage, but even these require a period with minimum watering during which the plant rests. With one exception, all of the plants discussed are members of the Amaryllis family.

Clivia *(Clivia miniata)*. Clivia, a native of South Africa, is a classic beauty with bold, colorful flowers that appear in late winter, but its foliage is attractive year-round. It has broad, strap-shaped leaves of shiny dark green, which grow about 18 inches long and arch outward in a thick clump. The flower stem rises two feet tall and is crowned by a cluster of funnel-

Clivia blooms in late March, early April. (Widmer)

shaped, two-inch blossoms, which form a rounded inflorescence, five to six inches in diameter. Flower color is typically orange with yellow centers. There are also varieties with yellow, soft orange, or red flowers, but they are harder to find.

Unlike many tropicals, clivia's foliage remains dense and deep green even in its resting stage. It is usually sold as a potted plant, since its root is not a true bulb but a fleshy root. Clivia blooms best when root-bound and can remain in a pot for many years without division. When plants do become crowded—literally overflowing their container—they can be repotted in the spring after they finish flowering.

Plant clivia in deep containers to allow for root growth. A potting mix of one part peat moss, one part good potting soil, and one part coarse sand or perlite is recommended. Add approximately two teaspoons of 5-10-5 fertilizer to the mix for each pot. During the winter months, place clivia in a bright location such as an east, south, or west window. Find a cool spot; temperatures in the low 60s at night seem to work well. Usually by late March or April the plant is in bloom.

In the summer, clivia can vacation outdoors in semi-shade with abundant water and monthly applications of a balanced fertilizer. In the fall, the amount of water can be reduced and the plant should be allowed to go through a rest period. Withhold fertilizer through the winter and resume around mid-March.

Blood Lily *(Haemanthus katharinae).* This plant derives its name from the red stains on its large white bulbs. The blood lily is a South African native with blooms up to nine inches across. The narrow-petaled blossoms are produced in umbels on thick stems. Myriads of thread-like stamens, tipped with yellow, protrude from each flower giving the umbel a showy, round, bottlebrush appearance. The leaves are glossy and wavy-edged, 12 to 15 inches long and 6 inches wide.

Bulbs should be planted in containers large enough to allow two inches between the bulb and the container sides, using the same soil mix as for clivia. Place bulbs even with the soil surface and set the containers in a warm spot with bright light, but not in direct sunlight. Water sparingly until the leaves begin to appear, which is usually in about eight weeks. Then water regularly throughout the growing and flowering season. Monthly applications of a balanced liquid fertilizer are recommended.

Towards the end of the summer, reduce the amount of water to encourage the leaves to dry. Trim off dry leaves, being careful not to damage the neck of the bulb. Blood lily can be stored in its pot by tipping the container on its side or by removing the bulb from the pot. The important thing is to store the bulb in a horizontal position.

Bulbs should be stored in a cool (50 to 60 degree), dry area. When it comes to time to repot, remove some of the old soil, and then repot in the same container. Move to a larger container only after several years when the bulb fills the pot almost completely. The blood lily can summer outside in a semi-shady location with plenty of water.

Cape Lily *(Veltheimia viridifolia)*. This South African native, a member of the lily family, not only has showy flowers but also attractive foliage. The wavy-edged, deep green, glossy leaves are about a foot long and three inches wide, growing in a fountain-shaped rosette. The flower stem is mottled brown and topped with an elongated cluster of drooping, tubular flowers in pale rose with yellowish-green petal tips.

Plant *Veltheimia* in the fall, in a container that allows three inches between the bulb and the pot. The bulb should be planted with the top of the neck exposed above the soil surface. A soil mix of one part each peat moss, compost, and perlite or coarse sand is recommended, with one to two teaspoons of a 5-10-5 fertilizer. Place containers in a cool location and keep the soil barely moist until growth begins.

As growth continues, increase the amount of water. Provide more light, higher temperatures, and fertilize every two weeks with a balanced liquid fertilizer throughout the growing season. Decrease water in late summer and let the foliage die. Begin watering when growth resumes in late fall. When containers become overcrowded, divide and repot in late summer.

Amaryllis *(Hippeastrum x hybridus)*. Not to be confused with the genus *Amaryllis*, *Hippeastrum* is commonly called amaryllis and is mainly native to tropical America. The Dutch hybrids, which are most commonly grown, are derived from species of Central and South America.

Each bulb produces one or two thick stems, each with a cluster of three to six trumpet-shaped blossoms up to nine inches across. Flower color ranges from white and light pink to brilliant shades of scarlet and crimson. Some varieties have contrasting veining. The leaves are light to medium green in color, strap-shaped and arching, rather than upright.

Start bulbs in late autumn or winter; the earlier you plant, the sooner the flowers will appear. Generally flowers appear four weeks after potting. Leave two

Amaryllis blossoms come in clusters of three to six. (Brown)

inches between the sides of the pot and the bulb. Use the same soil mix as recommended for clivia. Fill the container with soil, and plant the bulb so that the neck and top half of the bulb are exposed above the soil surface. Firm the soil and water well. Place the container in indirect light and warm (60 to 75 degrees) temperatures. Keep the soil slightly moist until growth begins.

Move to a sunny spot and water regularly during the bloom and growth phase. Apply a liquid fertilizer monthly until late summer. Taper off watering until the foliage dies down or yellows in September. When foliage is yellowed or dried,

carefully cut it and store the bulb or pot on its side in a cool, dry area. At planting time, replant in the same container using fresh soil.

Peruvian Daffodil *(Hymenocallis narcissiflora).* The flowers of this delightfully scented native of tropical America resemble daffodils in having two segments—the inner-forming a separate petaled funnel, and the outer, which are long, spidery, and recurved. The flowers are white with stripes of green in the throat and are found in clusters of two to five per stem. There are hybrids available in pure white and light primrose yellow. The leaves are medium green and strap-shaped.

Culture is very similar to the amaryllis. Pot bulbs in February, allowing a two-inch space between bulb and pot sides. Set the bulbs just beneath the soil surface. Place in bright light in a warm room and water lightly until growth starts. Water and fertilize monthly throughout the spring and summer; taper off watering in August. Store in September as you would the amaryllis.

Lily of the Nile *(Agapanthus africanus).* As its name implies, this *Agapanthus* is native to Africa. It is grown for its striking clusters of blue or white flowers. The nomenclature of this plant is rather confusing in that *A. africanus* is sold as

A. orientalis and both are sold as *A. umbellatus.* Good luck! In any case, these plants provide a heavenly shade of blue not commonly seen. The flowers are tubular or bell-shaped, borne in a round cluster or umbel. The blooms rise from attractive, fountain-like clumps of strap-shaped evergreen leaves.

Agapanthus flowers glow with a rare shade of blue. (Brown)

Agapanthus is generally available as a potted plant. It requires a dry, cool rest period during the fall and early winter. Its growth cycle and culture is similar to clivia. Water occasionally, keeping the soil on the dry side throughout the fall and early winter. Increase watering in February through March.

Fertilize throughout the spring and summer months with a balanced liquid fertilizer. Lily of the Nile requires bright light indoors. In the summer the pot can be placed outdoors in a semi-shady location.

A few final words about growing these amazing plants—the healthier and greater the vegetative growth, the more food is manufactured and stored for bud development. Failure to flower can be related to several factors, but the most common are poor vegetative growth during the growing season or inappropriate storage. Storage should be within the recommended temperatures; too cool or too warm can disrupt flowering. When storing bulbs during their dry resting stage, it is important to tip the pot on its side if stored potted. Many complaints relating to lack of flowering seem to be related to whether the bulb was stored upright or on its side. For the most effective rest period, the bulbs prefer to be dug out of the containers and laid on their sides.

All of these bulbs will flower better when their roots are a bit cramped in the pots. Indulge and enjoy these exotic and brilliant forerunners of summer. With a little care, they will bring color and brighten many a winter's day for years to come.

Chapter 5

Appendices

Mail Order Sources

Zone-Hardiness Map

About the Authors

Mail Order Sources

NAME OF COMPANY	TYPE OF MERCHANDISE	REMARKS
Stokes Seeds, Inc. Box 548 Buffalo, NY 14240	All kinds of seeds; good selection	Good all around source, excellent cultural advice, excellent source of vegetable seeds
Park Seed Co. Cokesbury Rd. Greenwood, SC 29647	All kinds of seeds, good selection, unusual garden perennials	Good all around source, excellent cultural advice, house plant seeds
Harris Seeds 961 Lyell Ave. Rochester, NY 14606	All kinds of seeds	Very reliable, good source for vegetables
Thompson & Morgan P.O. Box 1308 Jackson, NJ 08527	All kinds of seeds	Good source with an English flare
Farmer Seed & Nursery Faribault, MN 55021	All kinds of seeds & nursery stock	Local source, very reliable
Antonelli Brothers 2545 Capitola Rd. Santa Cruz, CA 95062	Tuberous begonia seed, tuberous begonias & gloxinia	Very reliable
Gardener's Supply 128 Intervale Rd. Burlington, VT 05401	Innovative garden equipment & gadgets	Very reliable
Van Ness Water Gardens 2460 N. Euclid Ave. Upland, CA 91786	Water lilies, bog plants, pond equipment	Excellent catalog
Burpee & Co. Warminster, PA 18974	Seeds, bulbs, plants, nursery stock	Very reliable
Heritage Gardens 1 Meadow Ridge Rd., Shenandoah, IA 51601	Garden perennials, vines, fruit trees, shrubs, shade trees	Reliable local source
Busse Gardens Rt. 2, Box 238 Cokato, MN 55321	Good variety of garden perennials	Good local source for all perennials
Ambergate Gardens 8015 Krey Ave. Waconia, MN 55387	Unusual garden perennials, Martagon lilies	Good local source for garden perennials
Borbeleta Gardens 15974 Canby Ave. Faribault, MN 55021	Daylilies, lilies, irises daffodils, Siberian irises	Good local source with excellent catalog

NAME OF COMPANY	TYPE OF MERCHANDISE	REMARKS
Van Bourgondien P.O. Box A 245 Farmindale Rd., Rt. 109 Babylon, NY 11702	Seasonal bulbs	Good source
Epicure Seeds Ltd. P.O. Box 450 Brewster, NY 10509	Unusual vegetables	European flare
Johnny's Selected Seeds Albion, ME 04910	Vegetable specialist	Good catalog with excellent cultural instructions
L. L. Olds Seed Co. P.O. Box 7790 2901 Packers Ave. Madison, WI 53707-7790	All seeds plus nursery stock	Good local source
Vermont Bean Seed Co. Garden Lane, Bomoseen VT 05732	Vegetable specialist	Good source, very unusual
Gurney's Seed & Nursery Co. 110 Capital St. Yankton, SD 57079	All kinds of seeds & nursery stock	Good source
Earl May Seed & Nursery Shenandoah, IA 51603	Seed & nursery stock	Good local source
Jung Seed Co. Randolph, WI 53956	Seeds, house plants, garden perennials	Good local source
North Star Gardens 19060 Manning Tr. Marine, MN 55047	Raspberry & blueberry specialist	Aimed at the market grower, good catalog
Jordan Seeds 6400 Upper Afton Rd. Woodbury, MN 55125	Vegetable seeds, market growers supplies	Aimed at the market gardener
Wilson Bros, Floral Co. Roachdale, IN 46172	Geranium specialist, African violets, fuchsia, begonias, house plants	Very reliable, good source
Donahue's Gardens P.O. Box366 420 S. W. 10th St. Faribault, MN 55021	Minnesota garden chrysan-themums, clematis, begonias, assorted hanging material	Excellent source for garden mums, local source with good quality
Prairie Restorations, Inc. P.O. Box 327 Princeton, MN 55371	Seeds for MN native prairie grasses & wild flowers	MN genotypes, locally grown

USDA Plant
Hardiness
Zone Map

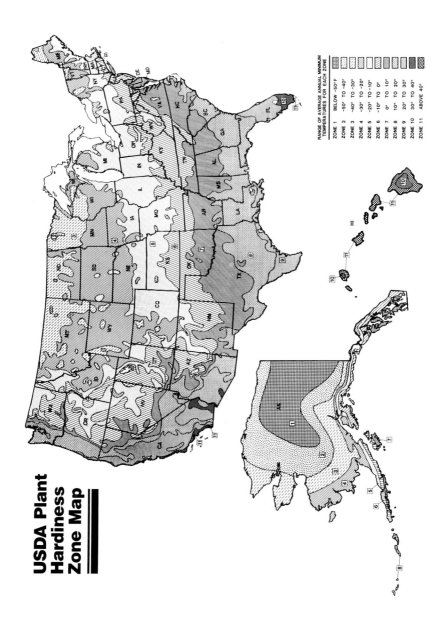

RANGE OF AVERAGE ANNUAL MINIMUM
TEMPERATURES FOR EACH ZONE

ZONE 1   BELOW -50°F
ZONE 2   -50° TO -40°
ZONE 3   -40° TO -30°
ZONE 4   -30° TO -20°
ZONE 5   -20° TO -10°
ZONE 6   -10° TO 0°
ZONE 7   0° TO 10°
ZONE 8   10° TO 20°
ZONE 9   20° TO 30°
ZONE 10 30° TO 40°
ZONE 11 ABOVE 40°

About the Authors

Diane Emerson is Past President of MSHS and gardens in St. Paul, Minnesota. Her own rooftop patio area sparked her interest in plants for balconies, decks, and patios.

Robert Estelle had a passion for container gardening, writing a regular column for *Minnesota Horticulturist* on plants, construction of garden areas, and growing methods for more than five years.

Fred Glasoe, Minneapolis, Minnesota, is a regular contributor to *Minnesota Horticulturist*, as well as the host of a weekly radio program on gardening. An avid promoter of gardening in the North, Fred is Past President of MSHS and a life member of the organization.

Judith Hillstrom shared her love of gardening through numerous articles in *Minnesota Horticulturist* until her death in 1989. Her work was published in *American Horticulturist*, *Better Homes and Gardens*, and other publications.

Bobbi Smidt Johnson writes from her home near Coleraine, Minnesota, which is in USDA hardiness Zone 3.

Dorothy Johnson is Executive Director of MSHS. As a volunteer in horticulture, she has been a Master Gardener since 1977 and is active in local and regional garden organizations.

Sis Kelm gardens five stories up where she has created privacy with trellises and moss-lined baskets.

Charlie King is an experienced northern gardener and Past President of MSHS. His container gardening expertise includes growing succulents and exotic tropicals.

Jim LaVigne is a nature photographer who enjoys capturing unusual floral specimens with his camera.

Emely Lincowski, formerly from Chisago County, Minnesota, is now a landscape designer in Pleasanton, California.

Robert Mugaas is an Extension Horticulture Educator in Hennepin County, Minneapolis, Minnesota. His hobby interest in northern rose growing has led him to share his insights through writing for *Minnesota Horticulturist*.

Philip H. Smith, a former MSHS president, wrote of his experiences planting entryway and deck spaces, and in using common land at the townhouse complex where he lived.